THE
STAKES
WERE HIGH

THE
STAKES
WERE HIGH

The Extraordinary Life of John Gully,
From Bruiser and Bookie to Fine
Old English Gentleman

KEITH BAKER

First published by Pitch Publishing, 2017

Pitch Publishing
A2 Yeoman Gate
Yeoman Way
Worthing
Sussex
BN13 3QZ

www.pitchpublishing.co.uk
info@pitchpublishing.co.uk

ISBN 978-1-78531-292-2

Typesetting and origination by Pitch Publishing
Printed in the UK by Bell & Bain, Glasgow, Scotland

Contents

Acknowledgements 6

Preface 8

1. The Early Days 11

2. Prize Fighting 18

3. Hen Pearce 30

4. Bob Gregson 38

5. The Racing World 48

6. The Blacklegs 65

7. The Lure of the Turf 78

8. William Crockford 88

9. Bob Ridsdale 100

10. Member of Parliament 111

11. The Danebury Confederacy 123

12. Lord George Bentinck 133

13. Running Rein 141

14. At Home 148

15. Robert Gully 163

16. Coal Mining 172

Conclusion 182

Bibliography 189

Index 190

Acknowledgements

JOHN GULLY was born on 17 August 1783, shortly before the first British journal to have *Sport* in its name appeared. When he died in March 1863 sports journalism had become a highly popular genre devoted to reporting on the impressive increase in sporting activities that had swept Victorian England. This book could not have been written without the sketches, accounts and reminiscences of the events and personalities of the age that have been left to us. My first debt of gratitude must therefore go to those sporting journalists and writers of the 19th century, starting with Pierce Egan, the leading boxing historian of the time, Nimrod (Charles Apperley) who covered the equestrian world, and to those vivid observers of the times – The Druid (Henry Dixon) and Thormanby (William Dixon), and Louis Curzon.

The Regency and early Victorian ages were a period of enormous change, extravagance, villainy and fraud, and have continued to attract the attention of modern sports historians such as Bernard Darwin, Henry Blyth, John Reid, Roger Longrigg, Michael Seth-Smith, and Nicholas Foulkes. I found their publications very informative when writing about various aspects of John Gully's career.

ACKNOWLEDGEMENTS

I am happy to acknowledge the professional assistance I have received from the staff of the following institutions – the British Library, (Boston Spa), and the Sheffield University, Pontefract and Ackworth Libraries. And to the editor Paul Camillin and others involved at Pitch Publishing who were involved in the preparation of this book.

Thanks are also due to the following individuals – Alan Grundy at the National Horseracing Museum, Hannah Gertig at The Jockey Club, Stephen Carlile at the Ackworth Heritage Group, and Jack Allen, author of *The Bristol Boys*. I am very grateful to Edward Baker for the insights he gave me into the world of bookmaking. Most importantly, special thanks are due to my wife Sarah for the constant support and encouragement given to me in writing this book and which I dedicate to her.

Preface

*'A most distinguished sportsman of
the Turf.'*

I N 1832 the young Lord Milton, heir to the earldom of
Fitzwilliam, came of age. As was the custom of the family,
a grand celebration to mark the occasion was held at the
family seat of Wentworth Woodhouse, near Rotherham,
Yorkshire. Invited to attend were all the notabilities of the
three Ridings of the county of Yorkshire, together with the
leading gentry and their wives.

Also invited were the Members of Parliament in the county
who had been elected at the recent general election, although
it has to be admitted that the Great Reform Act had brought
about representation of a large number of new members who
would have hardly been invited to Wentworth House as private
individuals. One new member however was there as a matter of
course since James Silk Buckingham, the flamboyant new MP
for nearby Sheffield, was well known as a world adventurer,
author and social reformer – just the sort of company Lord
Milton was very happy to greet.

Buckingham later described it as the most splendid occasion
he had ever witnessed. The enormous eastern facade of the

mansion, twice as long as Buckingham Palace, was one blaze of light. The great park itself was also brilliantly illuminated, and from nine in the evening until midnight a succession of carriages wended their way up the drive to the mansion.

Lord Fitzwilliam stood at the head of the staircase at the entrance to the marble saloon to receive his guests, to all of whom he had something kind or complimentary to say. The festivities were to continue throughout the night, the company departing only in the early hours of the morning.

Some 2,000 guests had assembled dressed in their gayest and finest clothes. There was, said Buckingham, 'a blaze of diamonds and jewellery, especially on some of the elderly ladies, whose natural beauty having departed, was sought to be replaced by artificial attractions, in which rouge, false hair, and other auxiliaries were used to harmonise with an openness of neck and bosom that was anything but appropriate'. [1]

But his gaze soon came to be drawn to a group of three people in particular. As they passed from room to room, he noticed they were shown special attention. The central figure was a handsome man with a fine, well formed and graceful looking figure, and resting on either of his arms were two of the loveliest women of all the assembled multitude. They were about 18 to 20 years old and dressed in plain green velvet, without a single ornament or jewel of any kind, 'but with such exquisite figures, blooming complexions, bright eyes, and rich and abundant hair, as might make either of them a worthy representative of the Venus of Cnidus, of Medicis, or of Canova.' [2]

Buckingham's curiosity was heightened by the fact no one seemed to know who they were or where they came from, and yet were receiving just as much if not more attention, from Lord Fitzwilliam as any other guests. At length, from

---

1   Autobiography of James Silk Buckingham, 1855, p.246
2   Ibid. p.247

discreet inquiries, it came to light that the gentleman's name was John Gully, a former prize fighter and the new Member of Parliament for Pontefract, and he was present with two of his daughters.

The news came as a great surprise to James Buckingham for he suddenly recalled that some 25 years earlier he had met the same man in much different circumstances at a small public house, The Plough, in Carey Street, Lincoln's Inn Fields in London. He had gone there to pay tribute to a popular young bare-knuckle fighter who had just become the undisputed champion of England by beating Bob Gregson in a terribly bloody fight.

Buckingham remembered seeing Gully as a tall, handsome young man of about 21 years of age, his head fearfully battered, cuts all over his face, and both eyes barely open. He was struck at the time by just how agreeable and gay in spirits Gully was as he celebrated his latest triumph. Wearing a little white apron, he had served his visitors with whatever drink they wanted, while his young wife, described by Buckingham as 'an exceedingly pretty woman though of the St Giles's style of beauty', assisted him in a most smiling and gracious manner.

Buckingham was even more astonished to be told that the same John Gully had not only reached the exalted position of Member of Parliament for Pontefract, but had acquired a great fortune as 'a most distinguished sportsman of the Turf'. Moreover, he was making a name for himself as the owner of several Durham coal mining collieries. He and his wife were now moving in the best of society, and lived nearby at his Ackworth Park estate, in a style of some elegance.

1

The Early Days

'Gully, fight me. It will make your fortune'

VERY little is known of John Gully's early years. He was born on 21 August 1783 to Richard and Susanna Gully at the Crown Inn in the village of Wick in Gloucestershire. Richard was the innkeeper of the 17th-century building in the village, which still occupies a prominent position on the London Road, although the inn is now called the Rose and Crown.

John had a younger brother and sister and their father soon found that running the inn provided only a meagre existence and was insufficient to support a growing family. He decided to move the family to the nearby town of Bristol, believing that he had better chances of success by becoming a butcher there.

Bristol, by the middle of the 18th century, had become England's second biggest city. Industry and the population were booming and it was the major port for trade with the American colonies and the West Indies. However, Richard's butcher's shop failed to thrive. Whether he lacked the skills to make a success of his shop, or it was poorly situated, is not clear. Moreover his health was not good and he died suddenly of a heart attack when John was only 13. John, as his eldest son, was left to run a business that was clearly in trouble. It was never going to work. Lacking a proper apprenticeship, John knew little of the trade and had never taken much interest in the shop. A lively and energetic lad, he was much more concerned with sporting activities.

Growing Up

He grew into a fine strong young man, described as being around six feet tall with rather an open and ingenuous countenance and with beautiful hands, of which all his life he was extremely proud. He was soon taking an active part in a number of sports and he would have been well aware that the Bristol and Bath area had at that time become the cradle of British bare-knuckle fighting. It could boast of producing several champions of England, known as the 'Bristol Boys'. They included fine fighters such as Ben Brain, Jem Belcher, Henry Pearce and the great Tom Cribb.

John would have taken the opportunity to see and learn more about boxing, particularly by attending the local fairs where various physical contests, notably boxing, were often the main attraction. The most important of all was the notorious St James Fair held in the heart of Bristol. It was the largest of the Bristol fairs and the annual week-long occasion attracted a great deal of trading, business and amusements in the numerous stalls and booths in the streets around the church.

For many ambitious young pugilists anxious to make their mark, the boxing booth would have been a prime attraction, since it was always crammed full of wealthy aristocrats and sportsmen from London, keen perhaps to spot another champion fighter. Whether John actually fought at the St James Fair is not known, but it seems very likely he would have found the penny entrance fee to view the bouts and learn something of the skills involved. He may well have tried his luck in an occasional bout or two at other smaller fairs which were a feature of the age.

He seems to have learned fast for there are a number of recorded incidents that suggest John had become very handy indeed with his fists. Some are clearly apocryphal. For example, after the criminal celebrity and highwayman – '16 String' Jack Rand – who weighed some 18st, had beaten a much lighter opponent called Bill Hooper, the 'Flying Tin Man of Bath', at Lansdown Fair, he then boasted he would send anyone else home in a cart if they so much as had the courage to fight him. Young John, after a word with his family, was said to have thrown his hat in the ring, and it was the unfortunate Jack who had to be carted away after being battered into submission. A rousing story but hardly a genuine one since Jack was hanged in 1774 for his crimes before Gully was born.

More credible is the account of Gully soundly thrashing a big bully at Bristol for unfairly setting his dog at a bull which he and his gang were baiting. Gully was pleased to hear later his defeated opponent was in fact a prize fighter who was something of a terror in the neighbourhood. And on another occasion John came across a number of ruffians torturing a dog and John was so incensed at the sight he went in with fists flying and managed to scatter the gang who fled into the night. Incidents like that would have whetted his appetite to try his hand in the prize ring.

However, with the butchery business still failing to prosper, John and the family were soon in deep financial trouble. He was clever with figures but knew very little about important aspects of the trade, such as sourcing and buying good meat, cutting, boning and trimming the meat, and striking a good bargain. He had no one to turn to as the debts grew and the creditors were demanding to be paid.

He was faced with the problem that even if he sold the business and the house, he would still be unable to settle all his debts. Moreover, John, barely 18 years old, also had a wife to support. In July 1801 he married a pretty local girl called Mary Mealing, a little older than himself, at the old church of St Thomas a Becket in the village of Pucklechurch, near Bristol.

At the age of 22 Gully decided to go to London. It is possible that he made the journey in response to a legal summons concerning the sums of money he owed. A more probable explanation was that Gully went to London without any definite objective in mind beyond a hope to try to restore his fortunes and at least escape the attention of his creditors back at home.

Whatever the reason, he had no success and soon had to admit to the authorities when they apprehended him that he was simply unable to settle his debts. He declared himself bankrupt, and 1805 found himself languishing in the notorious Fleet Prison in London.

Imprisonment

Bankruptcy in Georgian England was regarded as a serious offence. The Fleet Prison, together with the King's Bench and Marshalsea prisons in Southwark, were reserved exclusively for debtors. A prison term did not alleviate a person's debt, and an inmate was typically required to repay the creditor(s) in full before being released.

Wives and children were sometimes forced to join their husbands and fathers in prison if they did not have the means to support themselves, but there is no record of that happening with Gully. The likelihood is that his new wife Mary had not accompanied John to London and remained resident in Bristol with family members.

The Fleet Prison had a very poor reputation and was regarded by some as something of a 'hell hole' from which many never regained their freedom. It usually contained some 300 prisoners. Since debt was a classless offence, many people from all sections of society could find themselves confined there.

From what we know of his subsequent career, Gully was a resilient character, but as a callow young man he must have been dismayed by the strange and sorry company he now found himself mixing with. There was the 'cleaned-out gambler, the dissipated spendthrift, the debauchee, the extravagant, dishonest and fashionable tradesman, the pretended merchant, the pettifogging lawyer, the fraudulent bankrupt, the bold smuggler, the broken-down captain, the rogue, the fool, the schemer, the swindler, the hypocrite, the well-meaning but unfortunate gentleman'. [3]

Although conditions were undoubtedly overall harsh, some of the rules at the Fleet at that time were relatively relaxed, compared with other types of prison, probably more through mismanagement, than design. Visitors and tradesmen were allowed to mix freely with those imprisoned and at times it seemed just like a public house. On Monday night there was a wine club, and on Thursday night a beer club, each lasting usually until one or two in the morning.

With plenty of time on his hands, Gully made good use of the recreational activities available at the prison to keep him fit and active. Games of skittles and fives were played by the prisoners in the courtyard and Gully may well have even tried his hand at rackets which had become a popular pastime in both London's Fleet and King's Bench prisons. But it was the opportunity to practise his boxing skills by friendly bouts with other inmates that appealed most.

He soon made quite a reputation for himself and the word seems to have got round both within the prison and among visitors that he was a young man with real promise as a strong and brave young fighter. It was not long before the news

---

3   Thormanby. *Famous Racing Men*. p.73

reached a man also from Bristol – a successful prize fighter called Henry Pearce. It is possible that Pearce may have met John earlier and knew something about him, but in any event he decided to visit the prison to see for himself just how good this young Gully was as a budding fighter.

The Game Chicken

Henry 'Hen' Pearce had become nationally a very popular bare-knuckle fighter, 'a splendid figure in many ways' and widely known in sporting circles as the 'Game Chicken'. He had a relatively short but spectacular career and was said to have shot across the boxing horizon like a meteor and to fall extinguished just as fast. [4]

The Game Chicken is the first of a succession of remarkable sporting characters and eccentrics we shall meet in this book – drawn from princes and lords, gamblers and bookies, boxers and jockeys, racehorse owners and trainers – whose paths were destined to cross with John.

How long Gully may have languished in the Fleet Prison is impossible to say, but doubtless it would have been a good deal longer had not Pearce taken that momentous decision early in 1805 to make his visit to John at the prison.

Gully was pleased to greet his fellow Bristolian, and after some friendly conversation, he happily accepted the offer of some friendly sparring. A set of Broughton boxing gloves was available and the two men set to box over some good-humoured rounds. Gully acquitted himself remarkably well as a virtual novice and was able to lay a few good blows on the Game Chicken.

One account is that the experience alone was enough for Pearce, a veteran fighter who had something of a sentimental streak, to take pity on Gully's plight, and to remark to his

---

4   Downes Miles, Henry. *Pugilistica – The History of British Boxing.*
      p.167

muscular young opponent, 'Gully, fight me. It will make your fortune. I don't know which will win, but I think I may. Still, it is to be a very close and exciting thing.' [5]

Another more likely version, is that it took a number of other close bouts at the prison for Pearce and his patrons to hatch a plan for a prize fight between the two men that would not only extricate Gully from debt and prison, but which could also be promoted as a popular and lucrative bare-knuckle fight. Gully was surprised to receive such a proposal, but he needed little persuasion to agree to it.

As we shall see in Chapter 3, from then onwards events moved fast. Gully's release from prison was secured. News soon spread quickly around the sporting clubs and pubs of London that another promising young boxer from Bristol had been found and that a fine match was in prospect. Gully was about to venture into what was known as the noble art of bare-knuckle fighting or pugilism, which would lead eventually to him becoming one of the most famous sporting characters of 19th-century England. Before we turn to Gully's fighting career, it is worthwhile saying a little more about the sport itself which was about to enter its golden age.

---

5   Day, William. *Reminiscences of the Turf.* p.55

2

Prize Fighting

'In England, the FIST, only is used.'

THE roots of boxing lie deep in the past. It was an Olympic sport in 688 BC in ancient Greece. Even earlier, paintings on the walls of Egyptian tombs depict ancient Sumerians competing in boxing matches.

Undoubtedly, fighting with bare fists was a very tough, rough and brutal sport where serious injuries and even deaths sometimes occurred. Nonetheless it became a very popular sport in England from the late 18th century until the middle of the 1830s. It was during the Regency period of 1811–20 when it reached the height of its popularity.

It is often argued that the long and bitter struggle of the Napoleonic wars had created a sense of national doggedness and determination and this was reflected in the traditional masculine values demanded of prize fighters – tough and honest working-class men with bulldog courage, and never knowing when they were beaten. This manly spirit or bottom as it was known, was said to be a truly British art and was contrasted strongly with those countries where pugilism was unknown and the life of the individual might be in danger from slyer, more sinister means.

Thus it was claimed, 'In Holland, the long knife decides too frequently: scarcely any person in Italy is without the stiletto; and France and Germany are not particular in using stones, sticks, etc. to gratify revenge; but, in England, the FIST only is used.' [6]

The first documented account of a prize fight in Britain can be dated back to 1681 in the journal the *London Protestant*. Christopher Monck, 2nd Duke of Albemarle, arranged a fight between his own butler and butcher, with the butcher emerging victorious. As the sport developed, it soon became a much more fashionable institution. Bouts between hardy and determined young men would be arranged by wealthy patrons and a purse agreed upon. Side bets could be taken by the fighters themselves, by their entourage and by the watching crowds. These early boxing matches, mostly in London, were often ferocious affairs with no referee to keep order. They were more a test of strength and brute force than of skill and technique.

An important development occurred in the early 1700s when James Figg opened the School of Arms and Self Defence in London. Figg is acknowledged to be the first champion of the modern era. From 1719 to 1730, he had a little under 300 fights, winning every one of them. He brought into boxing some of the skills and movement derived from fencing and contests with quarterstaves and cudgels. The boxing school he set up was the first of its kind in the world and started the process of organising boxing into a coherent sport where trained athletes could compete against one another more by craft and punching skill than by ungainly wrestling and kicking.

---

6   Pierce Egan. *Boxiana*. p.13

However, despite Figg's efforts, prize fighting still lacked an agreed set of written rules which meant contests were still extremely disorganised and highly dangerous. It was not until 1743 that the first rules, called Broughton's Rules, were introduced to help regulate the sport and to get rid of at least some of its worst evils.

Broughton's Rules

Jack Broughton is considered to be the 'Father of the English School of Boxing'. He was an intelligent, well-mannered and communicative former boxer who drew up a set of rules designed to encourage fair play and the manly art of self-defence. Under the new rules, if a man went down and could not continue after a count of 30 seconds, the fight was judged to be over. Hitting a fighter while he was down and grasping below the waist were prohibited. Umpires were appointed.

The rules brought an element of order and respectability into the fighting scene and did allow the boxers at least one advantage not enjoyed by today's boxers. They permitted the fighter to drop to one knee to begin a 30-second count at any time and thus giving him an opportunity to recover. However, there was no limit to the number of rounds, neither was there any weight classification, so fighters of significantly different weights and physique were often pitted against one another.

The adoption of Broughton's Rules in London soon spread to other parts of the country and did much to eliminate many of the previous brutal practices associated with the sport. These included such savage practices as gouging eyes with fingers and thumbs, kicking a man with nailed shoes as he lay on the ground, hitting him in his vital parts below the waist, and seizing him when on his knees and hitting him until he was senseless. Broughton, it was said at the time, 'through his reforms had done more to establish the high character of

Englishmen for honour and fair play, than by all the eloquence of the pulpit or the senate'. [7]

To Broughton we also owe the introduction of gloves for sparring matches which enabled young boxers new to the sport to learn the skills without undue pain and injury.

However, despite the reforms, in the mid-1700s the sport suffered a period of decay due to the withdrawal of royal patronage, and from too many poor bouts, some of which were probably fixed anyway. There was a decline in the ability of boxers and a succession of champions who followed one another with 'the rapidity of the Emperors who followed Nero'. [8]

It needed a fine bare-knuckle fighter of the stature of John Gentleman Jackson (1769–1845), to revive the sport's reputation as a worthy and popular sport in England. Jackson held the title of champion of England after defeating Daniel Mendoza in 1795. He was the son of an eminent builder, with 'the character of a gentleman, equally respected by the rich and poor, and ever ready to perform a good action'. [9]

On his retirement, Jackson set about raising the respectability of the sport. He brought the sport out of the shadows, especially by cultivating the support of the aristocracy. He impressed everyone with his gentlemanly manners. He helped to set up fights, presided over inquiries into the conduct of bouts and even acted as a referee.

He founded an upmarket boxing academy at 13 Bond Street, London, which became very popular with the nobility and gentry, including Lord Byron. He insisted on teaching the scientific principles of boxing – countering blows, accurate judgement of distance, and agile footwork. The academy later became known as the Pugilistic Club and played a major part

---

7   Downs Miles, H. *Pugilistica*. p.26

8   Liebling, A.J. *The Sweet Science*. p.4

9   Pierce Egan. *Boxiana*. p.290

in arranging and running boxing contests as well as helping to raise money for prize fights.

The Growth of Pugilism

The era from the founding of Jackson's Pugilistic Club in 1814 to his retirement 1824 is generally regarded as the golden age of bare-knuckle fighting. It was still considered illegal under the terms of the Riot Act of 1715 as an affray and the bouts were sometimes hounded by the magistrates, especially within the city of London. However, this no longer deterred the bouts of popular champions like Gully, as well as Mendoza, Belcher, Pierce, and Cribb, from being openly patronised by the highest in the land.

The Prince Regent, later George IV, and his brothers the Duke of Clarence and the Duke of York were great supporters and regularly attended fights. The high status of the sport was confirmed at the coronation of George IV in 1821 when eight selected pugilists, selected by John Jackson, made up the guard to the entrance of Westminster Abbey (incidentally, John Gully was not among them but had retired several years earlier).

In particular, prize fighting had a great appeal for the wild and flamboyant group of aristocratic young bucks and upper-class sportsmen who characterised high regency society, the so-called 'Fancy'.

They had no formal clubhouse and often gathered in numbers in sporting public houses, especially in London, often managed by former prize fighters. Boxing has always had strong links with pubs and they played a crucial role in Georgian times as a place where sporting men who were not admitted to the exclusive London clubs, could meet and exchange gossip and news about forthcoming bouts and bet on the relative chances of the fighters. Some pubs might even stage bare-knuckle fights. The Lamb and Flag in Covent Garden had such a brutal reputation for pugilism that it earned the nickname 'The Bucket of Blood'.

The Fancy gambled and drank heavily and their evening would more often than not end with a chaunt – a sing-song tribute to a fighting man expressed in the form of a doggerel ballad (as we shall see, Gully was to become a particular favourite of the Fancy. They loved his courage – bottom – and his boxing skills). They were prepared to wager huge amounts of money on which fighter would draw first blood, to win a round or on the outcome of the fight.

At the height of its success, prize fighting was something of a social phenomenon. Championship fights would attract huge audiences of 30,000 to 40,000 people in a country of fewer than ten million inhabitants and in a pre-railway era when simply getting to a distant fight was extremely difficult. More often than not when a crowd arrived at the stated location of a fight, they found that an officer of the law had forbidden the contest, so the whole caravanserai would stream away to another place some miles away.

Fights would bring together a good cross-section of Georgian society – the wealthy and the poor, aristocrats and the gentry, men and women, and gamblers and crooks. They were in effect popular carnivals to be played out by a 'union of all ranks, from the brilliant of the highest class in the circle of Corinthians, down to the Dusty Bob gradation in society'. [10] The exception seems to have been the emergent middle class who saw the sport as little more than vulgar brawling.

There is no doubt that some of the spectators were animated by the possibility of witnessing some spectacular physical injury, and deaths still occurred well into the 19th century. But it would be wrong to think that all the fighters were brutally motivated by inflicting injury on their opponents. Most were

---

10   Reid, John. *Bucks And Bruisers.* p.17

incredibly brave and honourable men, who frequently showed concern for one another and gave their services to charity.

There was a strong regional element to the sport with cities outside London, especially Bristol, renowned for their prize fighters and whose wealthy backers made large contributions to the prize for the winner. The fame of the sport spread abroad. When the Russian Tsar and King of Prussia, along with the Generals Platoff and Blucher and their retinues, visited London in 1814 as part of a somewhat premature celebration of the defeat of Napoleon, they were impressed by the splendid sparring displays of Tom Cribb, Jem Belcher, John Jackson and other fighters.

Problems

The sport undoubtedly still had its problems. It had a close association with the criminal underworld which was particularly conspicuous during the Regency period. Swindlers, ruffians, crooked gamblers, thugs, bullies and pickpockets all lurked on the fringes of the sport. To some observers it seemed as if the crowd at some of the bouts 'consisted exclusively of the sweepings of the London slums and prisons'. [11]

Corruption too was common. Matches were still fixed, and fighters and referees bought off. Jem Ward, a bare-knuckle fighter and later heavyweight champion of England from 1825 to 1831, virtually wrecked his early professional career when he was heard in a bout to say to a much inferior opponent, 'Now, Bill, look sharp, hit me and I'll go down.' He was promptly hit and fell to the ground. He admitted taking £100, equivalent to several thousand pounds today, to lose a contest.

Unruly crowds were another problem. They might well have sought to bring a fight to a premature end if unhappy with how it was proceeding. One notorious instance was the first fight between Tom Cribb and Tom Molineaux on a

11   Ibid. p.137

bitterly cold and rainy day in December 1810 at Copthorne in Sussex. An overconfident and overweight Cribb was soon being outclassed by the black American Molineaux. The crowd was appalled that their English champion might be heading for a beating at the hands of a foreigner and a mob invaded the ring and disrupted the fight on a number of occasions.

Cribb was able to gain precious seconds to recover his breath until the ring was cleared. Gully, who by that time had become a close friend of Cribb and acted as one of his seconds, added to the outcry by complaining that Molineux had weights concealed in his fists. As it happened, eventually Cribb recovered sufficiently to wear the challenger down and to win in the 33rd round. But he had been taught a severe lesson. He would take good care that he was in much better condition when the return fight was held later in the following year and he was able to win comfortably.

Training and Captain Barclay

Preparing a prize fighter to be fit and strong enough for such long and brutal battle was a serious matter and demanded an exceptional training regime. Most bouts took place outdoors on bare ground and in all sorts of weather.

Without the benefit of protective gloves, fighters had to be very wary with their punch selection and would often circle and feint, or wait for an opportunity to secure a hold to help floor their opponent. Blows on the throat, the use of knees, elbows and finger jabs, though technically illegal, remained commonplace. Fighters had to be prepared to stay on their feet and endure punishment for long periods of time, and needed the wind to battle furiously in concentrated bursts. Consequently, the time fighters spent on training for a fight and perfecting their craft in the weeks and months before the bout, would often be the key to victory.

Few knew more about how a man should be prepared for an arduous physical feat than Captain Robert Barclay Allardice of Ury in Scotland. Generally known as Captain Barclay, he has a legitimate claim to be one of the most famous sporting figures of the period from 1800 to 1830.

He was a distinguished soldier, superb all-round athlete and successful gambler. Perhaps Barclay's main claim to fame came from the extraordinary feats he performed as a long-distance walker or what was known then as pedestrianism or professional racing. This was a most popular spectator sport in the late 18th and early 19th centuries and events attracted huge crowds. It was promoted and patronised mainly by the gentry and Barclay was its leading proponent. He would often walk 50 to 70 miles a day simply for pleasure, and as a runner he remained unbeaten over contests ranging from a quarter of a mile to two miles.

Captain Barclay was as strong as an ox, an avid fan of pugilism, and sparred regularly with the top boxers. He came to be regarded as the leading prize-fighting trainer of the time and any aspiring boxer would want to seek his advice. He laid down rigorous rules on how boxers should be best prepared for a fight and they were used widely by professional men and amateurs. The main ones dealt with exercise, sweating and feeding.

Regular exercise started in a fairly relaxed way but gradually increased in intensity. In full training, the boxer would have risen at 5am and his day would consist of two sessions of vigorous hikes of several miles, followed by running around a mile or two at top speed, all with the object of building up his body's stamina.

Two hours would be spent in the gymnasium doing skipping, rope climbing and exercises designed to develop all his muscles. The middle of the day was reserved for the sparring session, which would ideally last about an hour, when every possible scenario in the forthcoming fight was staged and planned for.

The remaining hours of the day were devoted to recovery through nutrition, sweating under piles of heavy blankets, massage and then a period of relaxation with conversation or games like cards.

Breakfasts and dinners would consist of fresh beef steaks, or underdone mutton chops, with stale bread and old beer. Too much liquor was thought to swell the abdomen and did not exceed three pints day. Milk was never allowed because it would curdle the stomach. Vegetables and fish were avoided as they were regarded as insufficiently nutritious (it has to be said that Barclay seems not to have adhered himself to such a rigorous training regime for he had a reputation for heavy eating and drinking). A boxer would have retired to bed about eight, and the next morning proceeded in the same way.

Gully admired Barclay and became one of his closest friends. Whether he actually underwent one of the rigorous training courses Barclay organised at his home in the Scottish Highlands is uncertain, but Gully would have taken careful note of Barclay's advice when preparing for a bout. We know that Gully was happy to take any opportunity to repay some of the gratitude he felt for the Captain.

In 1809 Barclay had made one of his famous bets with a Mr Webster, himself a sporting celebrity, that he could walk for 1,000 miles in 1,000 continuous hours for a bet of 1,000 guineas. The famous feat took place at Newmarket Heath over a 42-day period watched by huge crowds and Gully agreed to act as Barclay's bodyguard during his night-time walking. When Barclay successfully completed the last mile, it was Gully who led the crowd of more than 10,000 people in wild cheers. Barclay won the large purse, and a great deal more for those who had backed him, including no doubt, Gully himself.

The End of the Golden Age

From the mid-1830s onwards, there was a sharp decline in the popularity of bare-knuckle fighting, from which it did not recover. The withdrawal of royal and aristocratic patronage made it increasingly harder for boxers and promoters to defy the law. Its dubious association with the criminal world also did not help and matters got steadily worse.

The demise of John Jackson's Pugilistic Club removed a body of respectable and influential supporters who had acted as a sort of disciplinary and supervisory committee for the sport with the result there was a lack of a proper governing body to defend or reform it. As its former glory days and glamour faded, the Fancy themselves became disillusioned at the involvement of too many unsavoury characters in prize fighting. Moreover, the rising middle class was growing in influence, and their new temper of moral seriousness meant they regarded bare-knuckle fighting as low and degrading, and sought stronger measures to ban it.

The famous fight at Hungerford Down in 1821 between Bill Neat, the 'Bristol Bull', and Tom Hickman, known to the Fancy as 'The Gas Light Man', signalled just how much pugilism was in decline. Over 25,000 spectators watched the two men battle over 18 rounds. It was one of the bloodiest encounters in bare-knuckle history and the crowd was deeply shocked as the battered Hickman was reduced to utter senselessness. Public opinion thereafter moved quickly against the sport. The criminal law too was tightened up and as a result the authorities in the mid-to-late 1800s vigorously prosecuted the promoters of prize fighting and the boxers.

The last of the British champion prize fighters was Tom Sayers. In 1860 he fought the American challenger Peter Heenan at Farnborough over 42 hard-fought and savage rounds before the Aldershot police stormed the ring to stop the fight. The fight was declared a draw and Sayers dodged the police and returned to London to drink champagne at The Swan in the Old Kent Road.

He retired from prize fighting and died in 1865, just two years after Gully. Pugilism as a popular sport had by then become virtually obliterated and been replaced by the advent of a new era of boxing governed by the boxing rules introduced by the Marquess of Queensberry in 1867 which insisted on the use of padded gloves and a strict supervision on the type of blows permitted.

3

Hen Pearce

*'He must be a sharp chap, and
get up early, as beats John Gully,
I can tell you.'*

WHEN Hen Pearce, the Game Chicken, made that
important visit to John Gully at the Fleet Prison,
he was at the height of his popularity. Born in Bristol
in 1777, Pearce, like Gully, was apprenticed to a butcher and
started boxing as a boy. He would fight in contests set up for
bets by his father in local pubs and was, according to legend,
never beaten.

Pearce was a handsome, well-built man, and a fast and
skilful boxer who packed a punch with both hands. In a
championship decider, he defeated his fellow Bristolian Jem
Belcher in 1805 and remained champion until his retirement
in 1807 when he was succeeded by Gully.

He is considered to be one of the best champions in the
history of the British prize ring. Pierce Egan, the greatest
boxing writer of the time, described Pearce as, 'one of the most

heroic and humane Champions of England', and attributed him with godlike qualities, 'Almost Herculean, brave, noble and daring, generous and magnanimous.' [12]

Sponsors

Once Pearce and his backers were convinced that a match with Gully would draw sufficient interest, the next steps were to secure Gully's release, and to line up some prominent financial sponsors. Help was not long in coming. Mr Fletcher-Reid, a leading patron of the prize ring, had witnessed Gully sparring at the prison together with other Pearce supporters. He had a keen eye for new sporting talent and was impressed with Gully's potential. He promptly agreed to pay off Gully's debts – reported to have been around £300 – and secured his release from the Fleet Prison early in July 1805. Another very influential man who was also taking a close interest in the proposed bout was Colonel Henry Mellish.

Mellish was a very popular sportsman in Georgian England. He was a patron of many of the famous pugilists of the period, including Tom Cribb. He became a lifelong friend of Gully and one of his most prominent patrons. A fabulously rich man and a heavy and reckless gambler, he went through a fortune during his life. It was reported that he played for £40,000, or nearly £3m in today's money, at a card sitting, and that he once staked the same sum on a single throw of the dice, and lost. He loved the Turf, and at the height of his fame he once had 38 horses in training, 17 carriage horses, a dozen hunters in Leicestershire, four chargers in Brighton, and numerous hacks.

Gully was never to forget the opportunity Pearce and sponsors like Mellish and Fletcher-Reid gave him to start a new life outside prison. Nor did he forget the Fleet itself. The experience left a deep impression on him and helped mould his

12   Pierce Egan. p.145

determined character. He had seen at first hand the follies of men who had dissipated their fortunes by reckless, indulgent and foolish living. It was a lesson he never lost sight of. No one would take better care of his money than Gully.

With all the backers in place, Pearce and Gully were matched to fight for a prize of 1,000 guineas. Fletcher-Reid staked 600 guineas on Pearce to win, while 400 guineas was put down for Gully by Colonel Mellish. The bout was fixed for 20 July 1805 at Virginia Water in Surrey. Word seemed to have got round that Gully would be no pushover, and excitement was already running high, not least among the Fancy. To avoid any possible intervention of the magistrates, the organisers took care to keep publicity to a minimum and scheduled the fight to be over by 8am.

Gully's principal backers knew that putting a raw novice up against a hardened fighter and champion like Pearce was a huge gamble and might well back fire on them. Gully might last only a few rounds. They realised that there was simply not enough time before the bout for him to undergo the sort of rigorous and lengthy training regime offered by Captain Barclay in Scotland. Their best solution was to put Gully into the hands of the London trainer John 'Gentleman' Jackson, who we met earlier.

Jackson's first-hand experience of bare-knuckle fighting and reputation as a first-class trainer would have been well known to Colonel Mellish and Fletcher-Reid. For his part, Gully was determined not to disappoint his supporters. He was naturally a fit and strong man, and soon impressed Jackson with his readiness to learn the skills and craft of the boxing ring. It is likely that during that time Gully spent at Jackson's boxing academy, he may have sparred with Lord Byron who also attended it on occasions (it is reported however that the poet could neither punch nor defend himself very effectively).

The Fight

Early in the morning on the date fixed for the bout, a rumour swept round that the magistrates had after all caught wind of the fight and that officers with warrants were abroad. Not to be deterred, the whole of the cavalcade led by the Fancy in their coaches quickly made its way from Virginia Water on to Chobham some three miles away, where a ring had been put up.

A ripple of anxiety ran through the crowd when some, said to be in the know, began to raise concerns about the fight and some highly suspicious movement in the betting. A certain Mr Chersey had previously backed Henry Pearce very heavily a month or two ago but he was rumoured to have suddenly switched round and would now be backing John Gully, 'and by this no one could tell the enormous money he could win'.[13] There was a good deal of murmuring and grumbling in the crowd as they disputed over whether the fight should be allowed to take place.

It is not beyond the bounds of possibility that the rumour might even have been a calculated ruse by Gully's supporters to delay the date of the fight for two or three months, so as to give the rookie more time to prepare for it. Whatever the true reason, finally Fletcher-Reid thought it right to declare to the crowd that since the bets did not stand up to scrutiny, there should be no fight. In the event the discontented crowd were appeased by a fight between Tom Cribb and George Nicholls for a purse raised on the spot.

It was soon agreed that a new date for the fight would be Tuesday 8 October 1805 and it would take place at the small village of Hailsham in Sussex. Gully was thus given a couple of precious months or so to prepare himself. He trained hard, but was still raw and it is highly likely that Gully's sponsors would have used the time to draw on the training expertise of

13 Downs Miles. *Pugilistica*. p.173

Captain Barclay as well as Jackson to prepare their man for the bout.

The day of the fight dawned calm and bright, with just a touch of frost. It was just 13 days before the Battle of Trafalgar. Such was the pre-match hype about the fight, that a big crowd had gathered numbering some 10,000 people. It seemed practically all the sporting world was there. The Downs were covered with carriages and spectators of all the classes, including royalty itself in the person of the Duke of Clarence (later William IV) and the cream of England's aristocratic sportsmen.

At 1pm the fighters entered the 24-foot ring set up on a green next to the village to be greeted by a great cheer. Both wore the classic white knee-breeches and white silk stockings. Each wore his colours round his waist. Gully weighed 14st and had well-developed muscles. Pearce, at just over 13st, looked less impressive but was lean and fit. Colonel Mellish acted as the umpire.

It turned out to be a desperate and typically brutal battle of over 60 rounds from which both contestants emerged exhausted and badly battered. For the first seven rounds the champion had it all his own way, knocking Gully to the floor time after time. But then Gully overcame his nervousness and in the eighth round he landed a heavy blow and succeeded in knocking down Pearce for the first time. There were cheers for Gully and cries of, 'They are both Bristol men!'

The fight swayed back and forth with both men showing great courage and considerable science but Pearce seemed to be getting on top. Then in the 17th round Gully rallied with a series of hard blows which badly injured the Game Chicken's eye and put him down. The odds on Pearce winning fell to just 6/4.

In the following round Pearce was bleeding so profusely that both slipped over on sodden turf and virtually no fighting took place. By the 20th round it was Gully who appeared to be on top as Pearce's left eye was so damaged that he could hardly see. But in the 22nd round Gully was struck very hard, and while he was falling the Chicken hit him on the side of his head with such force that Gully vomited. Thereafter the tide turned in Pearce's favour and in successive rounds he landed punch after punch.

Both men were now bleeding heavily, Pearce from his eye and Gully from his ear. In the 44th round, Pearce hit Gully in his throat, and he fell like a log, temporarily unable to breathe. Thereafter, Gully continued to receive so many blows that he could barely stand and face his opponent. He had to resort to making a feint hit and then falling to the ground.

The fight dragged on relentlessly since it would only be ended if one side admitted defeat. But the punishment Gully was enduring was very severe, and after staggering on for a few more rounds he was reluctantly finally persuaded by his friends to 'fight no longer as the chance was against him'. [14] To his credit, among those who compelled Gully to give up was Colonel Mellish despite the fact that he lost a great deal of money since he had backed Gully heavily.

The fight had lasted 64 rounds and for an hour and 17 minutes. Both fighters were so badly injured that neither could see the other. Soon after the end, Pearce went up to his opponent to shake his hand and said, 'You're a damned good fellow; I'm hard put to it to stand. You are the only man that ever stood up to me.' [15]

Fame

Pearce and Gully had fought with great prowess and courage and emerged from such a tremendous contest with their reputations considerably enhanced. Both gained universal

14 Pierce Egan. *Boxiana*. p.165
15 Downs Miles. *Pugilistica*. p.175

praise. In a space of barely six months Gully had come from a paupers' prison to be a sporting hero and from now on a particular favourite of the Fancy. The Duke of Clarence, who had watched the fight at the back of the crowd on his horse, had risen with excitement at key moments in the fight and it remained thereafter one of his favourite topics of conversation.

Gully had to decide what to do with his hard-won fame. He was already showing the shrewdness and intelligence that would take him far, and Pearce's prescient remark about Gully after the fight was well-made and often quoted, 'He must be a sharp chap, and get up early, as beats John Gully, I can tell you.' [16]

He had experienced at first hand the physical dangers that accompanied the life of a prize fighter and was well aware it could be short-lived. On the other hand, there was fame to be had. He knew as well that he would not get a better opportunity to make some good money by fighting again and he was prepared to take the risk. His backers and supporters too were naturally keen to see him in the ring again.

However, Gully was in no hurry and it was to be some time before a challenger came forward. For the time being he was satisfied to become the landlord of a sporting house, in London – the Plough Tavern in Carey Street, Lincoln Inn Fields. His wife Mary and their young son Charles joined him there.

The Plough was popular with the London boxing and racing fraternity – the patrons and gamblers, and all the many hangers-on connected with sport. John and Mary proved to be a popular host and hostess. The conversation at the inn would inevitably turn to the important sporting events of the day, not least speculation over the chances of horses in forthcoming big race meetings. Gully, always respectful and a man of few words, may not have been drawn into the discussion, but he would have listened carefully to what was being said. Gully

---

16   Ibid. p.175

had some prize money to support his family and during his time at the Plough he felt confident enough to start betting on horses in a small way and even to take a bet or two himself. He initially seems to have had little success.

Money became short and for a while things looked bleak for him and his family. If he had aspirations to make a living as a betting man he must have realised that they might well not come to anything. On one occasion with barely a penny to his name, he sold his horse and set out to walk to Doncaster for the famous St Leger meeting where he hoped he might recoup some of his losses. Much of the journey was made on foot and he could afford to stay only at the cheapest of inns.

At Ferrybridge he was fortunate enough to be recognised by a prominent member of the Fancy – Mr Thomas Thornhill – probably one of the best judges of horse racing of the day. Gully gratefully accepted the offer of a lift for the last few miles to the course while balancing on the step of Thornhill's carriage. Squire Thornhill, as he was known, later became a member of the Jockey Club and the winner of two Epsom Derbys. He was just the sort of acquaintance Gully would successfully cultivate over the ensuing years.

As for Henry Pearce, after beating Gully his claim to being the champion of England was confirmed in December 1805 when he defeated Jem Belcher, one of the most popular and respected fighters seen in the prize ring. Belcher was one of the most naturally gifted fighters of his generation but unfortunately, when he fought the Game Chicken he was well past his best and had lost the sight of one eye when playing rackets. The fight took place on Barnby Moor, near Doncaster, and by the 18th round, Belcher was unable to move his left arm from his side. Finding himself totally disabled, he conceded the contest after fighting for 35 minutes.

4

Bob Gregson

*'Their brave hearts endeavoured to
protract the scene, reluctant to
pronounce the word ENOUGH.'*

TWO years had elapsed after Gully's fight with Pearce before he had his first challenge. It came from the north of England in the shape of a burly, 15st and 6ft 2in man called Bob Gregson, who had fought in Lancashire with much success. He was reckoned to be not as skilful as Gully, but had a longer reach together with great courage and prodigious strength. The contest took place on 14 October 1807, in a valley on the Newmarket Road called Six Mile Bottom.

The First Fight
Large crowds gathered at an early hour to witness the fight. Shortly after 9am Gully and Gregson entered the ring, both in excellent spirits and good condition. The bare-knuckle fighter Tom Cribb had become a close friend of John and was acting as his second. Bill Richmond, the famous black fighter and

former slave who had also been one of Lord Byron's sparring partners, acted for Gregson. The match was arranged for a stake of 200 guineas a side. When the fight started, the odds were 6/4 in favour of Gully.

There was some clever sparring in the first round as each contestant weighed up the other's strength but in the second Gully caught Gregson with a powerful right cross full on his nose which spattered the nearest spectators with blood and knocked him down. The next four rounds were fairly even, and then in the seventh Gregson at last managed to break through Gully's guard and landed a stunning blow on his eye, which was completely closed by the end of the round. The odds against him winning fell to 5/1.

Gully was left very much on the defensive in the eighth round when suddenly in an act of sheer power, Gregson caught Gully up in his arms and flung him to the ground. This was allowed according to the rules of the time and Gregson would also have been acting legally had he fallen on top of Gully, crushing him with his considerable weight. But to his credit he refrained from doing that, 'For which he was cheered by every spectator.' [17]

Over the next few rounds the odds continued to move in Gregson's favour as Gully seem to have weakened. His punches lacked force, and he took a lot of punishment to the head. But it remained anybody's battle and the betting became even. By the 25th round both men were dreadfully disfigured and utterly exhausted, 'like two inebriated men, helpless, and almost incapable of holding up their hands either to stop or hit'. [18]

The last ten rounds could hardly be called fighting. Both men were drained of all their strength and usually ended the rounds by rolling down to the ground together. 'Their

---

17   Downs Miles. *Pugilistica*. p.184
18   Ibid. p.184

brave hearts endeavoured to protract the scene, reluctant to pronounce the word ENOUGH.' [19]

Then in the 36th and last round, Gully, in one final and astonishing effort, hit his opponent with a blow to his chin which was just strong enough to prevent Gregson from getting up in time. He lay on the ground for some minutes unable to move or to speak while the elated Gully collapsed into Tom Cribb's arms.

The match was over but it was difficult to say which man was truly the winner. Such a gruelling and dreadful fight had rarely been witnessed before and it was reported, 'The bottom displayed on both sides excited universal astonishment.' [20]

Gully's stamina, skill and courage to overcome a man some two stones heavier and with such a long reach, filled the spectators and the wider sporting public with admiration. But it came with a cost. Gully's left arm had taken so many of Gregson's blows that it was permanently damaged, and the sorrowful mess of his face left him the more miserable sight of the two.

After the fight Gully was taken to rest in the carriage of Captain Barclay, who had become a close friend and patron. Despite their exhaustion and injuries, both fighters were fit enough to be present on the following day on Newmarket Heath where for a short while they were driven about to great applause. But it was Gully who stayed on the Heath for longer. It was as if he sensed that this was to be the place where much of his future life would be played out, rather than in the prize ring.

In 1807 Hen Pearce announced his retirement from boxing, as the champion of England, and returned to Bristol to be a publican. He had been champion for a relatively short time but his health became impaired. He had, said Pierce

---

19 Ibid. p.178
20 Pierce Egan. *Boxiana*. p.179

Egan, during his time in London, made rather too free with his constitution and in company with sporting men he frequently 'poured down copious libations at the shrine of Bacchus, added to the fond caresses of the softer sex, among whom he was a most distinguished favourite.' [21]

With Pearce's retirement from the ring in 1807, John Gully was generally recognised to be his legitimate successor as the English champion, although never formally nominated as such and Gully was careful not to claim the title. It was, nonetheless, an amazing turn of fortune.

Another Challenge

Less than a month had passed after the fight with Gully before Bob Gregson, encouraged by his friends, sent the following challenge to John, who was staying at the time with his parents -in-law in Hailsham in Sussex:

'Mr Gully – It is the wish of myself and friends that I should try my fortune with you in another battle, for £200 a-side. If you are inclined to give me this opportunity, I will thank you to say so, and also to name the time when it will be convenient to meet, to put down stakes, and arrange particulars. R. Gregson.'

The challenge placed Gully in a quandary. His financial position was much healthier after the previous fight and he had practically made up his mind to quit prize fighting. On the other hand, he was now acknowledged to be the champion of England, and was naturally very proud of the title. His sense of honour made it difficult for him to refuse a return match from a brave fighter who had so nearly beaten him a short time ago. He felt that the challenge had to be accepted. In his characteristic manner, he wasted no time or words in replying, 'Mr Gregson – I accept your challenge, but wish you would make for £250 instead of £200 a-side. I shall not

21   Ibid. p.151

delay a moment to returning to town to make the necessary arrangements as to time, place. John Gully.'

The Return Match

It was agreed that the fight would take place in May 1808, somewhere near Woburn on the border of the counties of Bedfordshire, Buckinghamshire and Hertfordshire. The organisers decided to keep the location and date secret right up to the last minute to avoid the magistrates getting wind of it. However, such was the interest, the news inevitably leaked and everyone soon seemed to be aware of the exact date of the fight – 10 May – and its proposed location. When the news reached the Marquess of Buckingham – a very fat nobleman, not unlike Sir John Falstaff – he was enraged.

He published a notice in the *County Chronicle* stating that he had been informed that a riotous assembly in the form of a boxing match was going to be held near the town of Dunstable, Buckinghamshire, on 10 May. He proclaimed, 'Proper steps had been taken for the detection and punishment of all persons acting in breach of the peace, by the attendance of the magistrates, high constables, petty constables, and other peace officers, entrusted with the execution of the law within the said county.' [22]

In fact, the threat did very little to dampen the enthusiasm for the forthcoming fight and merely added to the excitement. Large numbers of people left London over the weekend prior to be sure of securing beds and stabling in all the villages and hamlets near Woburn. By Monday there was uproar and chaos in the town with people of all kinds arriving on foot, on horseback, and in carriages of all description, all seeking accommodation which only a few could find.

To add to the confusion, the Marquess of Buckingham fulfilled his threat and all the region's constables and

22 Ibid. pp.180/181

magistrates were alerted, together with the local militia, the Dunstable Volunteers. The Volunteers had been founded to meet the possibility of a French army invasion, and were anxious to make a name for themselves. They had, it was said, 'grown tired of drilling when no Boney appeared, and were longing for an occasion on which they could display themselves'. [23]

Consequently, at the crack of dawn on that Monday morning, they marched through the town with drums beating, colours flying, and bayonets fixed. The citizens were shaken, supposing that the French had landed! As more and more people arrived on foot or with horses, the confusion reached such an extent that there were grave doubts as to whether the fight would ever be able to take place. The price of a bed soared to two guineas for a night. In one room in the town 15 gentlemen laid on the floor and hundreds had to sleep in their carriages.

Matters got even worse when the fight organisers suddenly changed the proposed location from Ashley Common to Sir John Selbright's Park in Hertfordshire, where Lord Buckingham's writ did not run. The trouble was that it was several miles from the spot first intended for the bout. Further mayhem broke out with a solid mass of confused passengers, carriages breaking down and obstructing the road, and broken-down horses who would go no further. Many hundreds of gentlemen were forced to be jolted along in brick carts hired for a shilling a mile.

Eventually the whole cavalcade succeeded in reaching the park and poured into it, churning and trampling the turf into a sea of mud. Nonetheless, the whole crowd behaved 'with tolerable decorum'. A reasonably firm piece of land was selected for the fight and a 40-foot ring was soon erected. Shortly before the fight was due to start another torrent of rain soaked

---

23 Darwin, Bernard, *John Gully and His Times*. p.27.

spectators to the skin, but spirits remained high. At 3pm the two fighters made their appearance, attended by numerous boxing heroes, such as Hen Pearce, Tom Cribb, Dutch Sam, Bill Richmond and others, all greeted with repeated cheers so much so that it was, 'impossible to describe the pleasure that beamed in the eyes of every spectator at this moment'. [24]

Gully and Gregson wore white breeches and white silk stockings and after an objection from Gully's supporters, Gregson removed his spiked shoes and both men fought in their bare feet. Captain Barclay was given the important role of umpire. Gully had trained hard and was so confident in his own abilities that a few moments before he entered the ring he offered to back himself for an additional £50.

However, after all the build-up, the high expectations aroused by the first fight between the two men were not fulfilled. In fact, Gully proved superior from the beginning despite the fact that his left arm had not recovered from the pounding it had received previously. He was far quicker and more skilful than the Lancastrian giant. He was able to evade Gregson's punches and was soon landing severe blows to his opponent's head.

By the tenth round both of Gregson's eyes were nearly closed, his nose broken and his face became a frightful mess. Although Gully went down, more than likely to take a rest, he was clearly on top and in subsequent rounds he was in complete command of the fight. In the 17th the frustrated Gregson rushed at Gully like a mad bull and tried to run his head into his opponent's stomach. Gully simply avoided him, hit him where he pleased, and when the wretched Gregson turned his back on his opponent and in panic made for the ropes, Gully followed him and pummelled him until finally letting his exhausted opponent slip to the ground.

---

24   Downs Miles. *Pugilistica*. p.188

Gregson, with great courage, refused to acknowledge defeat and fought on but continued to be severely punished. The 27th round decided the contest. Gregson was caught by a heavy blow under the ear and lay prone and senseless. He was unable to get to his feet for a further round. The battle had lasted for an hour and a quarter.

Retirement

Before leaving the ring, much to everyone's surprise including his prominent backers Captain Barclay and Fletcher-Reid, Gully dragged himself to the ropes and made a polite speech announcing that it was his decided intention to quit the ring. He thanked his patrons and told the crowd that he had not desired to fight at all and had wanted to follow the career as an innkeeper at the Plough in Carey Street.

He said he had felt honour bound to accept Gregson's challenge, and revealed that he had fought with an injured arm, and hoped that surely Gregson would not urge him to another combat. Gully then dressed himself, and was brought back in triumph to Dunstable in Lord Barrymore's barouche where he was the guest of honour at a select dinner of noblemen and gentlemen. Gully quickly recovered from the fight and was back at the Plough the following morning where he was to be seen, 'facetiously answering questions respecting the fight, and serving his numerous customers'. [25]

Despite the damage done to him, Gregson, brave as ever, decided to pursue his career as a prize fighter. The bouts he had with Gully, and later with Tom Cribb, are recorded in many publications in great detail and still rated in modern times as some of the greatest pugilistic battles of all time.

Gregson was in fact a relatively well-educated and cultured man with good manners and always dressed as a gentleman. He was also fond of poetry – sometimes referred to as the 'Poet

25   Ibid. p.189

Laureate to the Prize Ring' – and friend to Lord Byron. On retiring, he ran a London pub, the Castle Tavern, in Holborn, otherwise known as Bob's Chop-House, where he also set himself up as a bookmaker and fight promoter. The tavern was for a time effectively the headquarters of English pugilism. Unfortunately, Gregson was not a good businessman and left London for Dublin where he thought his particular talents were more likely to be appreciated. He died at Liverpool in 1824 the age of 46.

To sum up Gully's career as a prize fighter, it had been a relatively short one compared with other fighters of the time. He fought professionally only three times and never reached his full potential. But he is highly regarded among prize-fighting pundits as a 'most consummate pugilist'. [26]

Not a particularly big man at around six feet, he fought with a combination of science, quickness, hard hitting, and with a sheer fortitude rarely seen before his time. He had also demonstrated other virtues. He had shown himself to be an unassuming and intelligent person with good manners and a man able to gain respect and attention in all manner of circles. Nobody could accuse him of putting on airs.

He had resisted any temptation to sit back and simply bask in the adulation of crowds or become a mere plaything of the Fancy like Jem Belcher or Tom Cribb were prone to do. He had moreover learned the value of keeping his wits about him and making sure he was informed about anything that might serve him well for the future. Before his last bout with Gregson he had gathered inside information from someone close to his opponent about his training methods and a weakness he had in properly guarding his left eye against blows. Keeping well informed was to become a conspicuous feature of his later career.

---

26   Pierce Egan. *Boxiana*. p.186

Gully's career as a prize fighter was over but he did not entirely abandon boxing. He was happy to spar with other boxers and in the early years of his retirement he was also an active corner man, or second, to other fighters, notably his fellow west countryman Tom Cribb. The friendship between Gully and Cribb was to remain strong in subsequent years even though their lives followed very different courses. Gully also remained happy on occasions to make and take bets on the outcome of fights and was quite prepared also to act in that capacity for wealthy gamblers.

The history of prize fighting is full of stories about former fighters who on retirement were too prone to rest on their laurels, often running a pub, and then idle away their hard-won fortunes and fall into bad ways. Gully was determined to reach beyond that and had already plotted a way for it to best be done.

He had taken careful note from behind the bar at the Plough of the many stories of the escapades of the wealthy sportsman of the day, their reckless gambling and the fortunes being won and lost on the Turf. There was without doubt big money to be made from the gambling industry if a man was diligent and kept sharp enough. Shrewdly, he began to grasp the idea that both laying and making bets on racehorses might well offer a more profitable way of earning a living than keeping a public house.

5

The Racing World

'How delightful to see two, or sometimes more, of the most beautiful animals of the creation, struggling for superiority, stretching every muscle and sinew to obtain the prize and reach the goal!'

HORSE racing would become Gully's ruling passion – the source of his very considerable fortune and his rise in the social hierarchy. It was moreover a sport which was undergoing huge growth, innovation and popularity, and for adventurers like Gully, provided plenty of opportunities. To appreciate how Gully went about making his way in such a world we need to look more closely at what was going on.

It is of course one of the oldest sports in the world, known to have been popular with the ancient Greeks and Romans, Babylonians, Syrians and Egyptians as well as the nomadic tribesmen of Central Asia. And in China there are records of racing taking place in the Shang Yin and Han dynasties at a very much earlier time.

In England, there are accounts of horse racing during Roman times, and in the 12th century, racing is known to have taken place on public holidays at Smithfield in London, and at Chester, particularly on Shrove Tuesday. However, it was during the 17th century that flat racing first took a more organised turn. Its popularity increased especially amongst the aristocracy, thanks in particular to the royal connection. The sport flourished under Charles II and Queen Anne loved to go horse racing. She kept a large string of horses and as well as her Newmarket stables she was the first sovereign to attend courses in the north as well as the south. By the time George I came over from Hanover in 1714, horse racing was fairly well established all over Britain.

Thoroughbreds

The breeding and quality of good racehorses was the key factor behind the growth of the sport. This was due mainly to the import of the light and fast Arabian stallions from Turkey and the Middle East, which were then bred with the larger English mares to create the forefathers of the thoroughbred horses we see racing today. The three founding sires from which almost all thoroughbreds can be traced back to are: the Byerley Turk (1680–96), the Darly Arabian (1706–23), and the Godolphin (1724–53) all named after their respective owners, Captain Robert Byerley, Thomas Darley, and Lord Godolphin. Thoroughbreds weighed less than many other breeds of horse and stood out because of their delicate heads, trim bodies, strong chests and relatively short backs. They were also known for being rather highly strung. Above all, they had the size, stamina and speed to run very fast over different distances.

As racing and breeding became more popular and the number of thoroughbreds increased, there was a need for breeding information to be recorded so that their identity could be established. James Weatherby, an accountant of the Jockey Club, was assigned the task in 1773 of tracing the pedigree and family history of all thoroughbred racehorses in England. His work resulted in the *Introduction to the General Stud Book* being first published in 1791, and since 1793 Weatherbys have recorded, in the *Stud Book*, the pedigree of every foal born to thoroughbreds.

Newmarket in Suffolk became by far the main venue for horse race meetings and was soon recognised as the headquarters of English flat racing. It was closely associated with the Royalty, the aristocracy and upper classes. Although George III (1760–1820) took little interest in horse racing, his son the Prince of Wales was devoted as a young man to the sport and kept his own stud and raced his horses at Newmarket. The town features prominently in the life of John Gully and his family. He lived in or near the town for many years and it was there that his horse racing career began.

Match Races and Sweepstakes

Up to the 1770s the first horse races that took place on established English courses were mainly what were termed match races, between two or occasionally three owners each racing a single horse over a course of four or five miles for a stated prize or plate sometimes in the form of a silver or gold cup. One problem was that in a two-horse race, the winning owner provided half his own prize. Another was when several horses began to be entered for a prize this might involve multiple heats which took a long time to run and attracted few spectators outside the racing fraternity.

A further drawback was that a four- or five-mile race often turned out to be a lengthy dawdle followed by a desperate rush over the last quarter of a mile. It was clear that much more needed be done to make the sport attractive to spectators and to new owners. What was needed was more variety, with a greater number of shorter races offering greater opportunities to bet.

Consequently, the second half of the 18th century saw a major development when races began to be introduced which were made up of just a single field consisting of several horses. Gradually, the early emphasis on stamina was replaced by racing younger horses – two- and three-year-olds – who could race thrillingly over the ground at great speed. These races were funded mainly by a contribution from each owner, and the winner received all the combined stakes which had been put down on the race.

Each race now more often than not involved several horses giving spectators plenty of entertainment and, importantly, an opportunity of a choice of bets on different outcomes. Such events came to be called sweepstakes, to distinguish them from the former match races. The St Leger race at Doncaster became the first major sweepstake event to be limited to just three-year-old colts and fillies and soon proved very popular. Initially run in 1776 over a distance of two miles, it was later reduced to one mile and six furlongs in 1813.

The Oaks in 1779 and the Derby in 1780 followed, and were run over similar distances at Epsom Downs. With the introduction of Two Thousand and One Thousand Guineas at Newmarket in 1809 and 1814 respectively, this group of races established themselves as the Classic ones of the British Turf and wining them carried enormous prestige for their owners.

The handicapping of horses designed to give all horses an equal chance of winning by carrying different weights according to their form, was another development that found increasing favour among both owners and the wider public. The leading newspapers and sporting journals also began to give horse racing far more coverage. Consequently, by the end of the 18th century, horse racing had become much more popular and a major source of entertainment in many towns throughout Britain.[27] Its popularity had also opened up several new sources of revenue, and none more important than gambling.

Racecourses

Newmarket maintained its premier position for owners, trainers and the breeders of racehorses. It had more days of meetings than elsewhere and was extremely popular with all classes. When the horses were in sight, 'how delightful to see two, or sometimes more, of the beautiful animals of the creation, struggling for superiority, stretching every muscle and sinew to obtain the prize and reach the goal!'[28]

On a big race day the town of Newmarket might well contain half the British peerage at one end of the social scale, and at the other, hordes of scoundrels for a day or two had the place entirely at their mercy. A young German visiting the town on a racing day was left overwhelmed by all the activity. He exclaimed, 'The town appeared uncommonly animated. Trains of horses were led up and down the streets. Excellent equipages, gigs, curricles and tandems flew past each other. Jockeys were carrying saddles and bridles to and fro. In short, all was full of life and bustle. Horses were prancing about with the swiftness of an arrow. Newspapers, journals, and other means of entertainment are plentifully provided; and wherever we cast our eyes we see advertisements of sales of horses, descriptions of others for sale, and the name of Tattersall's, the famous London horse dealer, appears everywhere.'[29]

---

27 Huggins, Mike. *Flat Racing and British Society*. 1790-1914. p.18

28 Longrigg, Roger. *The History of Horse Racing*. p.88

29 Spiker, Samuel. *Travels through England, Wales and Scotland in the year 1816*. p.271.

Apart from Newmarket, regular race meetings also took place in towns such as Doncaster, York, Chester, Ayr, Lincoln and Brighton. But there were many smaller courses which might stage only one race a year, and were frequently associated with festive holidays and other entertainments. Although attendance was severely restricted by poor transport, these meetings were always extremely popular with the local communities.

They attracted relatively large crowds of working-class people drawn by their fair-like atmosphere, their numerous activities such as dicing, cockfighting, bare-knuckle fighting, the plentiful supplies of drink available, and the chance of winning some money. For example, before a railway line in South Yorkshire was opened, 'Sheffielders, man and boy, thought nothing, year after year, of walking through the night to Doncaster, taking up a good position next to the rails, which they never quitted from ten to five, and then walking the 18 miles home again.' [30]

It was down to the spread of railways in the 1830s and 40s, which fundamentally changed the nature of the sport from a predominantly local sport to much more of a national one. The first special services for horse racing were run by the London and Southampton Railway for the 1838 Derby. These special trains could now bring in crowds of people (and indeed horses) to the venue from several neighbouring towns and villages. Consequently spectator levels increased dramatically.

The impact of the railways on racing is famously illustrated in William Frith's painting of Derby Day, which attracted huge crowds when exhibited at the National Gallery in 1858. The picture depicts the annual spectacle of the Derby, when it was estimated half a million Londoners left town for the day to see the fleetest horses in the world. The canvas illustrates the extraordinary panorama of the sheer scale of Victorian society

---

30   The Druid. *The Post and the Paddock*. p.4

which was being attracted to the racecourse. The careful images of what are reckoned to be nearly one hundred distinct social types show just how popular the sport had become among men and women from all backgrounds.

Although the authorities in the 18th and early 19th centuries were somewhat fearful of large crowds, the large attendances at the principal racing events were not generally regarded as dangerous and a major threat to the peace. That said, racecourses certainly attracted criminal gangs of thimble-riggers (sleight-of-hand gambling games), pickpockets and ruffians who were liable to terrorise spectators, and sometimes fought pitched battles among themselves.

Doncaster had a particularly bad name and complaints were made about the growing number of ruffians who assembled there and which the magistracy seemed unable to ban or control. All early attempts to suppress their activities failed. In 1829 a troop of the 3rd Dragoon Guards had to be dispatched to arrest the ringleaders. The thimble men barricaded themselves on the town moor using stones and chair legs in an attempt to stop being driven off their favourite sites. Some 150 thieves, pickpockets and confidence tricksters were eventually rounded up and convicted. [31]

Owners and Trainers

In the early part of the 18th century, titled gentlemen and those from wealthy landowning backgrounds, tended to ride their own horses in match races as amateurs. They tended to race more for honour and recreation than for money. However, as the century drew on, the status of winning, higher prize money, and the growth of gambling, made the owning and breeding of racing horses a much more prestigious and potentially prosperous activity. The great aristocratic owners led the way and rivalled one another

---

31 Huggins, M. *Flat Racing and British Society 1790-1914*. p,135

to breed the best horses of the time capable of winning the premier races of the day

One of the greatest owners of the age was the 12th Earl of Derby, 1752–1834, who was devoted to horse racing, game-cock fighting and gambling, and had the Epsom Derby named after him in 1780 (there are numerous Derbys in existence today, including the Kentucky Derby, which are named after the Earl of Derby). Lord Derby had to wait until the Derby of 1787 before winning it with Sir Peter Teazle.

Lord Derby's great rival, the 3rd Earl of Egremont at Petworth, 1751–1837, had more success. His stud was the largest in England and horses from his stud won five Derbys and five Oaks as well. Later in the mid-1800s, Lord George Bentinck was another very famous owner and breeder, as well as being a prodigious gambler. In 1845 he won a total of £1m, a colossal sum for that period and worth over £115m today. He won every major race in England with the exception of the Derby. Shortly before he decided to abandon racing to go into politics, he sold a horse named Surplice which went on to win the Derby. He was heartbroken and exclaimed, 'All my life I have been trying for this, and for what have I sacrificed it.' [32]

Gradually, the ownership of racehorses spread more widely among the middle classes, notably the landowning gentry. It is difficult to make a precise estimate, but in the early 1800s when Gully was setting out on his career on the Turf, just over half of owners were calculated to be from wealthy middle-class backgrounds. [33] Yet there would always be some from relatively poor backgrounds who had ambitions to own a horse or two which would not only boost their social status, but might also provide a way of getting some useful inside stable knowledge.

The careful training and stabling of racing horses became a crucial business. As racing prospered, the majority of serious

32   Ibid. p.54
33   Ibid. p,78

racehorse owners came to accept that the key to success lay as much with a good trainer as with the jockey. To keep a horse in health demanded the unceasing attention of its trainer to see that its food and drink were of the best quality, it was carefully stabled, and that its gallops were properly organised. Perhaps above all the trainer had to be extremely watchful that no improper person had access to the horse. 'Sometimes, though a trainer be ever so lynx-eyed and careful, he will be baffled, and will awake to the sad consciousness, some fine morning about the time fixed for a race, that the horse has been got at by some interested party, and rendered useless for the coming event.' [34]

John Gully saw the emergence of some very successful and highly sought-after trainers, often celebrities in their own right, such as Robert Robson, the Emperor of Newmarket trainers, who had 33 Classic winners between 1793 and 1828. The Yorkshire-based John Scott had sole control of Lord Derby's stud and had a run of success in the St Leger which is unlikely ever to be beaten. 'Honest' John Day (the nickname was applied ironically) was regarded as the leading trainer in the south of England and horses trained by him won seven classics between 1838 and 1854. He was the senior member of a racing family that was 'highly effective and utterly unencumbered by morals'. [35] The Day family trained several of Gully's horses and often found themselves caught up in a number of the racing scandals of the mid-19th century.

Jockeys

In the early 1800s the wealthier owners might still employ grooms to ride their racehorses, but most owners had to resort to hiring jockeys who tended to hang around the main centres of racing, especially Newmarket. Those early jockeys were

---

34 Curzon, Louis. *A Mirror of the Turf.* p.88
35 Foulkes, Nicholas. *Gentlemen and Blackguards.* p.23

often scruffy and unkempt and were for some time not well-regarded at all. But with more and more big money at stake, owners and trainers became aware that the crucial difference between good jockeys and bad jockeys was their ability to give the horse a much better chance to win.

All horses have their own likes and dislikes; some like to lead, others to sit in the pack, some need to be ridden hard, while others are comfortable at the back. A good jockey can know how much energy the horse has left, and can push it right to the limit.

If a jockey performed consistently well, he soon became much vaunted by owners, and indeed rich and famous. A good jockey retained by a wealthy owner or trainer could earn as much as £1,000 a year or more, and petted like a prima donna. [36]

Jem Robinson (a six-times Derby winner) was said to have received 100 guineas just for riding Ephesus in the 1851 St Leger. But most jockeys had to rely on a mixture of agreed fees for riding a particular horse, and gifts or betting. Fees were low – around five guineas for winning one of the Classic races and just three for losing races – and might well be difficult to wheedle out of their patron. One rider, the precocious Jem Snowden who won the Oaks at the age of 17, and later the Derby and St Leger, claimed that on one occasion he rode seven winners at Ayr and received seven promises to pay and got nothing! [37]

However, Snowden was far from reliable himself. He once turned up for Chester Races a week late and his love of drink in the Yorkshire pubs was legendary.

In Georgian England, becoming a jockey was undoubtedly a tough and dangerous life and remains so today. High-spirited and very powerful thoroughbreds weighing on average 500kg

36 Curzon, Louis. *A Mirrow of the Turf.* p.268

37 Huggins, M. *Flat Racing and British Society 1790-1914.* p.161

and reaching speeds of up to 40 miles an hour are very difficult to control and accidents among the early jockeys were legion. Small of build, they had to endure long periods of fasting and vigorous wasting to keep their weight down to a minimum before the season started. Their diet had to be extremely frugal.

On a typical day, the jockey for breakfast would have a small piece of bread and butter with tea. The lunchtime meal might be a small piece of pudding and meat or fish, a little or no bread at teatime, but no food after. As to exercise, after breakfast jockeys would be loaded up with clothes – five or six waistcoats, two coats, and as many breeches. Then walks would be taken for ten or 15 miles in the heat of summer, and sometimes they collapsed from sheer exhaustion.

If they were able to stick to such a regime, jockeys could become as sleek and fit as the horses they were going to ride. The problem for them was that wasting of that kind could be quickly offset by a rapid accumulation of weight once they relaxed it – a jockey weighing no more than seven stone in peak condition could gain as many pounds in just a few days as had been lost. Once the racing season was over the jockey Francis Buckle, a hero of the Turf at that time, apparently liked nothing better than to sit down and have a whole goose for his supper.

John Gully, a good horseman himself, grew to know many of the jockeys well, both the honest ones and the ones not so honest. He respected their toughness and ability even though he distrusted some of them. He admired in particular the great Georgian jockey Francis Buckle, arguably the most famous jockey of the time. Buckle was an honest and respectable man, called 'The Pocket Hercules'. During a career that lasted 45 years he won a total of 27 Classic races.

There were others, too, who would have been well known to Gully for their characteristic riding styles and foibles. Sam

Chifney Jnr was a jockey famous for what was called his last-second Chifney Rush strategy. However big the field, he was almost certain to be among the last runners until towards the end of the race when he would sweep to the front with a fearful concentration of man and horse power. It was said that his fingers on the reins when a horse had a delicate mouth, were like a dancer's feet on a tightrope.

Another famous rider, Bill Scott, was the exact opposite to Chifney. He always strove to lead from the front in a race, setting a pace which would hopefully exhaust the other horses. A kind-hearted, heavy drinking and forceful jockey, he rode the winners of nine St Legers and four Derbys. He probably should also have beaten John Gully's Pyrrhus the First in the 1846 Derby if he hadn't been too drunk to keep his horse straight.

Gully, on numerous occasions, used Honest John Day and his extended family to ride for him. Sam and Alfred Day respectively rode two of Gully's Derby winners – Pyrrhus the First and Andover. Sam had the misfortune to break nearly every bone in his body, apart from his right arm. He was fond of holding forth to the young jockeys on the best way to lose weight. 'Drinking,' he would say, 'inflates you just like a balloon; champagne and light wines are all rubbish – they only blow a fellow's roof off. But no man can work if he can't eat; you can't get light without eating – have a good mutton chop, that's my style.' [38]

Fraud and deception

With ever-increasing sums of money at stake, and lacking a strong regulatory authority, horse racing became prone inevitably to fraud and deception. The first tentative steps to deal with the problem were taken early in the 18th century when Parliament passed an Act in 1740 specifying that horses

38   Thormanby. *Famous Racing Men*. p.62

entered had to be the bona fide property of their owners so as to prevent ringers, that is a superior horse entered fraudulently in a race against inferior horses. Horses also had to be certified as to age and for rough riding jockeys were penalised.

However, by the early 1800s various corrupt practices had become widespread involving owners, trainers, jockeys and even the officials. Betting by trainers and jockeys was a particular evil of the time. No owner would feel himself secure if a trainer or jockey was betting against the very horses with which they had been entrusted.

In addition, the sport was prone to several other accusations of bribery and corruption. Additional weights could be hidden on a horse to slow its pace. On the actual racecourse, jockeys could be bribed to upset their rivals by claiming a false start, or deliberately bumping another horse, especially the favourite, out of the race, and so on. The jockey Harry Edwards was among the finest riders of Gully's time, but too easily tempted by some of the more croked ruffians of his day. It was said that he would rather make a pony by nobbling a horse than get a hundred by other means, so thoroughly did he enjoy doing a bit on the quiet on his own account, and 'putting the double edge on the swells'.

More seriously, horses were being maltreated, doped and in some cases, poisoned. One of the most infamous examples occurred late in the 18th century. The jockey Sam Chifney Snr was the retained jockey of the Prince Regent and a very fine one. But he was another who had a reputation for dishonesty. It was said that Tattenham Corner – the turn into the straight at Epsom racecourse – was straighter than Chifney! On 20 October 1791 Chifney rode the Prince's horse, Escape, at Newmarket in a 60 guinea race over two miles. He started as a 2/1 favourite but finished last of four.

The next day, at much improved odds of 5/1, Chifney won a race over four miles on the same horse. Immediately some ugly rumours broke out. Some people suggested that the Prince had nobbled his own horse by giving it a bucket of water before it ran on the 20th. Others thought that Chifney himself had deliberately pulled Escape in the first race in order to improve the odds and thereby make a financial killing in the second race. In the end nothing was proved but the circumstantial evidence and Chifney's dubious character suggested otherwise, and his career ended in ignominy.

Another notorious scandal occurred in 1811 when Dan Dawson, a quiet, red-faced stable lad at Newmarket and a well-known tout (a racing tipster), was found to have poured arsenic in the water troughs used by three of his stable's horses. Some shady bookmakers had taken big bets on the three horses and had hired Dawson simply to incapacitate them. But he used far too much arsenic and the horses died.

After a high-profile trial, and despite strenuous efforts by one of the owners – Lord Foley – to save him, Dawson was hanged for his crime in 1812. Shortly before he went to the scaffold, a group of his friends drove over from Newmarket to say farewell to him. They unexpectedly came across Dawson, blindfolded, in the jail yard on his way to the scaffold. His last words to them were, 'Good bye; God bless you! my Newmarket lads; you see I can't shake hands with you. Good-bye!' [39]

Betting

Although a few of the aristocrats and the upper classes might have run their horses simply for the honour and prestige that came with winning, for most people the appeal of the Turf lay with betting. As a contemporary, the Druid (Henry Hall), commented, 'The Turf would stricken and droop without betting, as completely as commerce and business without speculation.' [40]

---

39   Druid. *Post and The Paddock*. p.168
40   Ibid. p.59

Even the frugal Admiral Rous, the so-called 'Dictator of the Turf', argued that betting was a necessary adjunct to racing, and without it, 'Four fifths of the racecourses would be ploughed up.' [41] The Admiral was the most influential Jockey Club steward in the middle of the 19th century, effectively running horse racing in England for around 40 years. Like all men of strong character and individuality, he had stiff opinions and was not easily persuaded that they could possibly be wrong.

Besides his reservations about gambling, the Admiral had a strong aversion to tobacco, believing that half the ills of modern flesh could be traced to the use of 'that vile and pernicious weed'.

In the early match races between just two or occasionally three horses, the rival owners who were drawn mainly from the upper class would bet between themselves often for large sums of money. The most notorious so-called plungers did not shrink from having £5,000 to £6,000 on a single match. Colonel Mellish, for example, one of the heaviest of bettors, lost £20,000 on the Sancho–Pavilion match at Lewes in 1804, although it was noted that such trifles did not 'weigh very long on a philosophic mind like the Colonel's'. [42]

It was the introduction of the sweepstake races in the late 1770s that led to major changes in the nature and scale of betting. With larger fields to bet on, these races proved to be far more exciting and interesting than the traditional head-to-head races. Crucially, they enabled punters to have a choice of bets on different outcomes and at different prices. This was a crucial development for as we shall see, it prepared the way for the emergence of the professional bookmaker who saw the opportunity to make a living out of betting.

Fixture lists containing the names of the horses in future races gave another boost to the betting industry. They were

---

41 Huggins, M. *Flat Racing*. p. 54
42 Longrigg. R. *The History of Racing*. p.116

first introduced for the Classics and meant that a horse could be bet upon in a race some months before it occurred, perhaps even as a yearling. Previously most betting had to be done in a club or at the racecourse betting post on the day of the race. In effect this allowed the development of a futures market to be created, now known as ante-post betting. It allowed prices to be quoted sometimes far in advance at very long odds and though a most risky business, it did enable some very big winning bets to be made.

It was a gentleman and racehorse owner by the name of Richard Tattersall who played the key role in the emergence of ante-post betting. In 1776, 'Old Tatt' as he was known, had founded Tattersall's, a horse auction market in a rural situation near Hyde Park Corner on the outskirts of London. He was probably the first breeder of thoroughbreds to sell his young horses rather than race them. His honesty and businesslike dealings attracted the attention of the nobility and wealthy sporting and betting men from the gentry, and his premises soon became a popular gambling rendezvous for them.

Tattersall fitted up two rooms or subscription rooms, where members could make their wagers, and settle any outstanding debts in comfort on a gentlemanly basis off-course. Although Tattersall's remained well into the 19th century as the principal centre in Britain for ante-post betting transactions, similar betting facilities for the upper classes soon became available elsewhere, such as the exclusive London clubs, and notably Crockford's in the heart of Mayfair.

However, as regards betting on horses among the working and middle classes, until the early 1800s there were virtually no similar facilities for them to bet off course and their betting was restricted to where and when a race meeting took place locally. Since there were not yet bookmakers in the true sense of the word, bets had to be made between individuals or with gangs of men, many of whom were often little more than the sharpsters and swindlers who made a trade of setting on young and inexperienced men.

The usual place where bets could be struck was at a simple post (a betting post) on the racecourse where those prepared to take on a bet would congregate. At Epsom the place chosen was opposite the grandstand but moved to the crest of the Downs where it formed around a gibbet. On big race days, it was said to be utter confusion – 'a mixture of dukes and dregs, exactly like a cockpit.' [43]

But as Carl Chinn, a leading authority of betting has pointed out, it would be a mistake to underestimate the amount of money that could be staked on those occasions. Gambling could be heavy and wherever a race meeting took place it would be frequently accompanied by lots of other gambling activities such as cards, dice and cockfighting.

To sum up, in the first half of the 19th century, horse racing in Britain had enjoyed a spectacular period of growth. A good deal of improvements were still necessary but going to the races with all their clamour and excitement, fairs and amusements, and excessive eating and drinking, had clearly become a very popular and important form of entertainment. And as we shall see in the following chapters, it was betting which would remain at the heart of it all. The scene was set for John Gully to take his place as the most audacious and successful bookmaker of his times.

---

43   Ibid. p. 117

6

The Blacklegs

'Of the public racing men at Newmarket, Messrs Crockford, Gully, Ridsdale, Saddler, the Chifneys, etc., we need not say much, their deeds being almost always before us.'

The Birth of Bookmaking

'Had there been no bookmakers', said John Gully, 'the Derby never would have become what it is.' [44] In racing terms, bookmaking is the tally of the amounts of money bet on each horse in a race and the betting odds necessary to ensure a profit as far as possible on whatever the outcome. The skill of the bookmaker therefore is to vary the price of each horse to attract (by offering longer odds) or deter (by shortening the odds) wagers to ensure a balanced book and thereby achieve a profit.

If a large bet was made, the bookmaker could lay off some of the risk by hedging bets with other bookmakers. In other

---

44   Curzon, Louis. *The Blue Riband of the Turf.* p.170

words, a market of both sellers of bets and buyers is established. Needless to say it could be a risky enterprise, and any would-be bookmaker had to be able to think on his feet and be calm under pressure. On the eve of a race, especially when large sums of money were being wagered, the rise and fall of the odds could be dramatic. But as we shall see, it was a craft that perfectly suited the likes of Gully.

The idea of laying and taking bets professionally for a living has roots that can be traced back into the 18th century to some notorious gamblers such as Captain Vernon, Col. Denis O'Kelly and Dick England. All were basically adventurers and barely trustworthy, and would not be recognised as bookmakers as such. But they shared a common characteristic, notably a willingness to be more systematic and careful about balancing the risks involved in taking and making wagers. Vernon in particular appreciated the concept of covering himself by hedging his bets, that is betting on both sides of an event to minimise the risk.

The escapades and dubious characters of men like Vernon, O'Kelly and England were disapproved of by many of the upper classes who branded them as little more than turf swindlers and rogues. Unfortunately, that reputation stuck to anyone who sought to make an honest living out of betting and thereby ensured that when the craft of bookmaking did emerge at the beginning of the 19th century it was tarnished as a bad and deceitful occupation.

Some say that it was a Lancastrian named Harry Ogden who was the first of a new breed of bookmakers to abandon all the former systems of betting and introduce the one essentially we have today. One day late in the 1790s, he announced to the punters at Newmarket Heath that he was prepared, much to their surprise, to offer a price against each one of the horses in the next race. It proved very popular and it was not long before others like him followed suit. This practice was at first called betting around and then later, making a book. It was to signify the beginning of the age of the professional bookmaker.

The Rise of the Blacklegs

The first group of men who can legitimately be called professional bookmakers appeared in numbers on racecourses around 1804, and were very different from the aristocratic gamblers of the past. They were drawn heavily from the working class. Because of their background, they were initially virtually all excluded from all the upper-class betting Rings which featured in the late 18th century. Those Rings usually consisted of around 100 or more wealthy men, most of whom would be racehorse owners.

It was essentially a system whereby gentlemen were making bets with other gentlemen. But it was a narrow and restrictive process which depended to a large degree on trust and good will. In practice, gentlemen, even of the highest character, might well cheat one other or go bankrupt, and not be able to meet their commitments. As horse racing boomed, what was badly needed was a much more businesslike arrangement, and one offering a much wider range of people prepared to take bets.

Consequently, from 1800 onwards those gentleman betting Rings began to be joined by a much more proletarian group of bookmakers. At first they were treated with suspicion and lack of respect and branded in racing circles as swine, wager ghouls or blacklegs. The pejorative term blackleg was typical of the class prejudice of the time, and its origins are not entirely clear.

Some say it was derived from the black boots worn by some of them, or perhaps even from the rook with its black legs. Others argue it stemmed from the action of some of the rogues who ran away when they could not pay their debts. Whatever the reason, those early working-class bookmakers or legs, as they were soon commonly called, had a low status to start with and had to struggle to make a living. In time, however, they came to be accepted by the gambling fraternity and regarded as the true fathers of bookkeeping.

At first they were made up of a relatively small number of men, who sensed the expansion of gambling on horses offered an opportunity to earn a regular and possibly a lucrative living. They were prepared to take bets or to back horses themselves, or if they were fortunate, to act for others as commissioners (agents) for wealthy gamblers. With their coarse accents, unattractive appearance and rough and rude expressions, those early legs were easy to ridicule.

Many were drawn from touts, grooms or those who hung about the racing and livery stables. Several were virtually illiterate and barely able to write their names or read a race card. But they were more often than not sharp, quick-witted and invariably had a head for figures with astonishing powers of mental arithmetic. No doubt they had among them their fair share of crooks and swindlers, but most were trustworthy and civil enough and eager to do business.

Another attraction for the working man was that bookkeeping was an open occupation, not restricted by apprentice regulations, rights or privilege. They might well be sneered upon as ignorant lower-class upstarts but on the Turf their money was as good as anyone else's. The majority were ready to lay generous odds when they thought it opportune, and crucially they paid up when they lost.

Moreover, the more thoughtful legs, and Gully is a prime example, were not inherently greedy, and quite prepared to offer odds allowing a small percentage of profit as long as they were getting a large turnover. Those legs who made a reputation for honesty, good judgement and straight dealing, could bring them into direct contact with the wealthiest sportsmen of the day. No one saw that more clearly than Gully. Their mere word, said one noble gentleman, 'is better than other men's bonds', and when they lost a bet they paid out five, ten or £20,000 without the slightest hesitation. [45]

But those early blacklegs had to work very hard for their money. The number of racecourses was growing fast, they were constantly on the move and much business had to be got through almost every day of the year. It was vital that they kept themselves up with the current racing form of horses.

Many undoubtedly fell by the wayside, but in a relatively short time those that had their wits about them did very well out of their new occupation and amassed handsome fortunes. Their success was aptly summed up by Nimrod – a contemporary racing expert – when he wrote, 'Of the public racing men at Newmarket, Messrs Crockford, Gully, Ridsdale, Saddler, the Chifneys, etc., we need not say much, their deeds being almost always before us. But looking at the extraordinary results of these men's deeds, who will not allow racing to be the best trade going? Talk of studs, tales of winnings, talk of racing establishments…are but the beings of a summer's day, when compared with those illustrious personages, and their various transactions and doings on the Turf.' [46]

Those early legs were truly an extraordinary bunch of men and it is worthwhile looking briefly at the lives of some of the more unforgettable ones. Characters like Crutch Robinson, Jem Bland, Jerry Cloves, Harry Hill, Robert Ridsdale, William Crockford, and above all John Gully, had a huge influence on the betting scene and on their contemporaries. Since we shall have more to say later about Crockford and Ridsdale, they can be left aside for the moment. Suffice to say, both were destined to feature prominently in the racing career of John Gully.

---

45 Curzon, Louis. *A Mirror of the Turf.* p.224
46 Quoted in Whyte, James Christie. *History Of The British Turf: From the Earliest Period To The Present Day.* pp.615/616

Jem Robinson

Perhaps the best known and most respected amongst the early blacklegs was Crutch Robinson, said to be a 'democratic leg, who loved to fleece a noble'. [47] He was a little, decrepit, and wizen-faced man, disabled and dependent on a crutch, but held a unique place among the sporting characters of the age. He relished making money out of the upper-class, wealthy gamblers, or swells as they were known, and would accept bets as great as £1,000 on a horse.

Not much is known about him beyond the fact that he was from a poor background. He had probably been a stable boy somewhere, and his lameness had most likely come from the kick of a horse. But if anyone mentioned his lameness he would raise a sneering smile of reticence. His ability to make complicated mathematical calculations in his head and his craft were so good, that he seldom lost money on a race. He never gambled himself and thought himself somewhat above the other legs. He was respected as an honest and intelligent man. His interests were wide-ranging and he was said to be as knowledgeable about politics as about horses.

However, he had his critics. His very success went down badly with some of his rivals, who depicted him as a domineering, uncouth being who was 'blanched by time, shouting out the odds and dealing in bitter sarcasm and racing slang, either mounted on a four-legged brute as rough as himself, or leaning on his trusty crutch in the midst of the crushing throng, and was an irreverent and disgusting sight'.[48]

By the middle of the 19th century Robinson had disappeared from the racing scene and was thought to be dead. He seemed to have passed away in a lonely old house in Manchester. It remains a mystery as to whether he was married

---

47 Jem Robinson. *Dictionary of National Biography*
48 Sylvanus. *The Bye Lanes and Downs of England.* p.127

or had children, or what happened to the vast fortune he must have amassed.

Jerry Cloves

Jerry Cloves was for a while recognised as the would-be leader of the blacklegs. He had the advantage of being a gentleman's gentleman and claimed to be well connected with the upper class. He had a booming voice and liked to orchestrate affairs on the betting Ring and on the racecourse. When large numbers of the legs gathered for whatever business was afoot, very likely Jerry would be there to be their spokesman.

We have been left a vivid description of one such scene. At Brighton during the Lewes races, the legs and gamblers used to gather on the Steyne at an early hour to commence their operations on the first day. 'The buzz was tremendous, until Lord Foley, and Mellish, two of the greatest gamblers of the day, would approach the assembled betting Ring, and then a sudden silence would ensue to await the opening of their books. At last Mr Jerry Cloves – presumably the principal bookmaker of the period – would say, "Come, Mr Mellish, will you light the candle and set us a-going." Then…the whole pack opened, and the air resounded with every shade of odds and betting.' [49]

Jemmy Bland

Perhaps the most notorious blackleg of the times was Facetious Jemmy Bland, described as 'an atrocious leg of the ancient, top-booted, and semi-highwayman school'. [50] Although his physique was not in any way like a highwayman – he was short and flabby – he certainly dressed like one with his white beaver hat, cutaway coat with large brass buttons and a huge double-breasted waistcoat and white cord breeches.

---

49 Spencer, Edward. *King's Racehorses: a history of the connection of H. M. Majesty King Edward VII with the national sport*. p.7

50 The Druid. *The Post and The Paddock*. p.55

He and his brother Joe had learnt about horse racing while first working as post boys and then as livery-stable keepers in Wardour Street in London. He was coarse, unkempt and almost illiterate, although his wife eventually managed to educate him enough to sign his name in a virtually indecipherable scrawl. Eventually she taught him to use a kind of hieroglyphic shorthand which in his later days enabled him to successfully record bets although they still needed a lot of deciphering.

Bland was undoubtedly a hard, remorseless man who it was said would have willingly sold his father over a racehorse or put his foot upon the necks of a whole generation if it had been in his interests. As early as 1811 Jem and his brother Joe were among those suspected to being linked to the infamous Dan Dawson scandal which cost the lives of four racehorses and which was to reduce even John Gully to tears.

Bland's deep, raucous voice was often heard bellowing out the odds across the Ring at racecourses. Some of his betting exploits became legendary. Perhaps his greatest coup was in the St Leger of 1826 when he won over £30,000 by betting at 25/1 on a horse considered to have no chance.

That was followed soon after by the famous Plenipotentiary scandal of 1834. Plenipo, as he was known, had won the Derby earlier in the year at a canter and had been made a hot favourite for the St Leger. But he lost badly. Described as 'light and bounding' two days before the race, he was 'gross and helpless' when he came to the starting post. Clearly the horse had been got at. Rumours went round that the owner of Plenipo was in league with Jem Bland to fix the race but it is unlikely that the owner would have agreed to lose such a prestigious race. However, most people thought Bland had somehow done well enough out of the race to secure the purchase of his fine mansion in Piccadilly. [51]

51 Thormanby. *Famous Racing Men*. p.27

Just two years later, Jem met his nemesis in the shape of the Duke of Cleveland, nicknamed the Jesuit of the Turf or Slippery Sam, and probably as astute a bookmaker as any of them. Cleveland was more than a match for the craftiest of legs and he vowed that one day he would break their betting Ring of which Bland was a leading member. He very nearly succeeded when he is reputed to have taken £80,000 (approximately £8m today) from Bland on a horse called Shillelagh. Bland was rarely seen again on the Turf, but still died a rich man.

Ludlow Bond

Bond was another well-known bookie though not so coarse in style as many of his contemporaries. Very ambitious, he allowed himself to be appointed the nominal owner of some racehorses whose real ones belonged to a body called the Yorkshire Blacksmith Co. They had such a shady reputation that no one else would back a horse known to be theirs! Ludlow at times appeared on Newmarket Heath on a grey hack which earned him the sinister nickname of Death on the Pale Horse. He was, in fact, no more than a mere puppet without exactly knowing who was pulling the strings. The whole affair was discreditable but Ludlow rather gloried in it. Determined to see that his status as a racehorse owner would not be forgotten, he christened a yearling which he bought from the Duke of Grafton as Ludlow Junior.

Harry Hill

Harry Hill had started his career as a boot cleaner in a Manchester hotel before deciding to go into business on his own.

He got involved in gambling by touring the racecourses and fairgrounds as a clever exponent of gambling deceptions, like the thimble and pea and the three-card tricks, whereby gullible bettors could be tricked of their money by sleight of hand. Fear of jail kept such small-time tricksters from travelling from one town to the next, never staying in one place very long. But Hill soon took up betting on horses in a more serious way.

Despite his lack of education, dirty appearance and vulgar wit, he had a common sense and astuteness about money, and managed to win the confidence and praise of some eminent backers. He eventually rose to a position of considerable trust on the Turf as a betting commissioner for the wealthy. Lord George Bentinck in particular, who knew a great deal about horses and racing, took a liking to him, and entrusted Hill with his commissions, many of which were the largest commissions ever entrusted to a racing agent.

Hill also became a close friend and partner of Gully. As partners they pulled off several major betting coups, some by very dubious means. However, unlike Gully, Hill never had ambitions to lead the life of a respectable country gentleman. No amount of money or contact with upper-class men could wean him from the tastes of his early days, notably, the inn-yard and the tap-room. It was said that he was never so much at home as when, 'He presided at a table surrounded by ostlers, jockeys and the nondescripts of the Turf, from which he himself had sprung. There he was the king. Everybody roared at his queer stories, which were quite unfit for ears other than those of the men who surrounded him; and the louder they roared the more drinks he stood.' [52]

Given the prejudice and rigid class structure of the times, it is not surprising that legs like Robinson, the brothers Bland, Hill, and indeed Gully, were for several years looked down upon and ridiculed by some of the landed and upper class as little more than low-born louts, offensive, and a 'parasitical scum'. [53]

---

52 Ibid. p. 27

53 Foulkes, N. *Gentlemen and Blackguards*. p.56

It is likely that there was an element of self-interest in doing so because their pockets were being hit hard by the exploits of their working-class rivals. A strong case can be made for arguing, as one authority has done, that the baiting of working-class legs as cheats and rogues was motivated more by jealousy of their success and by the bigoted view that, 'because a man was a bookmaker he must therefore be without honour, without scruple, without any true sportsmanship and willing to adopt any means to make money.' [54]

However, by the 1830s attitudes were changing fast. A significant expansion in working-class betting had taken place and the sport had become more open with the advent of the telegraph, better transport and greater press coverage. Middle-class bookmakers appeared, attracted by the profits that could be made from the sport. Moreover, two prominent legs in particular – William Davies and Fred Swindell – did much to enhance the reputation of those early bookies. Both were widely praised in the racing world for their integrity and were men who had steered well clear of the worst excesses of the betting Rings.

Davies was a carpenter by trade who made a name for himself as the first of the so-called breed of honest bookmakers. He was another one who had a genius for the manipulation of figures. Said to be a man of unimpeachable character and high moral standards, his betting contemporaries acknowledged, 'His unassuming deportment and unwavering probity of conduct during his career on the Turf…have earned him golden opinions in every sense of the word.' [55]

Much to the consternation of those who still had a low opinion of the legs, Davies early in his career publicly demonstrated his integrity when he lost £10,000 on a handicap race at Newmarket but immediately paid up his losses in sparkling and crisp £1,000 notes!

---

54   Chinn. Carl. *Better Betting*. p. 48
55   *Illustrated London News*. 1 June 1850. p.386

Such was the patronage he gained from many of the heaviest backers of horses, that he became known as 'Davies, The Leviathan'. Just like Gully, Davies always took good care to ensure that the interests of his clients were looked after. He did not approve of credit and when he took a bet which proved successful, his clients were assured of their winnings without any waste of time. He died in October 1879, aged 61. By his will he left property in railway shares valued at £60,000 to the Brighton Corporation.

Fred Swindell was another who proved to be a popular and highly respected leg. He was a Derbyshire labourer who from the age of 12 had worked as an engine cleaner. He went on to use his hard-earned savings to build up a thriving business as a bookmaker.

Appreciated for his discretion and integrity, he succeeded by the 1850s in also becoming an important betting commissioner. He worked for some of the greatest owners of racehorses of the age such as James Murray and Sir Joseph Hawley. He also died a very rich man.

The reputations of Davies and Swindell, together with other working-class legs of their ilk, made it difficult for those who still persisted in deriding them to sustain their attacks. By the 1840s the abusive terms attached to them had virtually diminished. Their status and role as leading practitioners of the craft of bookmaking were recognised by their presence in the so-called betting Rings. This meant that instead of having to do business at betting posts around the course, they now more often gathered together in parts of the main stand of a racecourse.

Those occasions had a reputation of being very noisy and boisterous at times. When in 1839 one of the stewards at Doncaster argued that the arrangement 'caused annoyance to the ladies', it was agreed by the town council to place the bookies and punters in a railed-off lawn away from the more exclusive enclosures. This soon became the standard practice at other race courses. [56]

Of all those early bookmakers, Gully stands out as the most impressive and successful – in the space of a decade or so he rose to become the doyen of them all. Very few were able to compete with the fortune he made from racing and the status he achieved. It is now time to look in more detail at his career on the Turf and the secret of his success.

---

56   Chinn, C. *Better Betting*. p. 49

7

The Lure of the Turf

*'He knew how to
worship the rising sun.'*

JOHN Gully had good reasons for his decision to turn to
horse racing as a career. First, he genuinely liked horses,
and quickly developed an instinctive judgement about
their ability which was to stand him in good stead throughout
his time on the Turf. He loved the buzz and excitement of the
racecourse and the thrill of the gamble. Importantly, he also
had the right attributes for a bookmaker – a sharp, shrewd
and calculating mind. He was aware, too, that horse racing
attracted the same kind of wealthy gentleman gamblers who
had supported him earlier as a prize fighter. They might, he
considered, well look favourably on his new occupation if he
could win and retain their trust.

The First Steps
It seems very likely too that Gully's wife would have been
pleased when he decided to retire from the ring. Being married
to a prize fighter carrying the risks of a serious injury cannot

have been pleasant for a young wife. At the same time she also had to contend with bringing up their growing number of children. Her life would not have been easy.

Gully's work as a blackleg bookmaker had got underway around 1808 and he was beginning to spend a good deal of his time away from home in Newmarket on building up his betting business. This left the Plough Inn largely in Mary's care. Eventually as John's racing activities began to prosper, he felt sufficiently well off to employ a manager to run the inn, and to acquire a three-bedroomed town house nearby for his family. However, it was soon simply not big enough to accommodate all of them plus the office space he needed for his work.

The family therefore decided around 1812 to give up the Plough and move to permanent lodgings at Newmarket. The property was well and tastefully furnished, and Gully was beginning to make sufficient money to ensure the family could enjoy a comfortable and respectable lifestyle. They were able to entertain regularly. Gully, it was said, 'was a generous host who served his friends with no sparing hand, passing the claret and slicing the pines, as if he had been foaled at Knowsley or Bretby', [57] (the residences of Lord Derby and George Stanhope respectively, both famous and wealthy racehorse owners).

In one important respect Gully was fortunate for he was beginning his career as a bookmaker just when betting was beginning to be recognised as a proper business. Moreover, it was an age of very heavy betting, that is, there were 100 or so of the Turf who betted in stakes of hundreds or thousands of pounds. He started off modestly enough and for a while was quite content to mix freely with other legs and to take or make bets from anyone who wished to do so.

From 1810 until 1827 relatively little is known about all of Gully's activities. However, it is clear that he was fast learning the tricks of the trade and building up a very good reputation

---

57 Downs Miles, *H. Pugilistica*. p.191

as a top bookmaker. By now he had come to the conclusion that simply backing horses was an unprofitable business and that the best way to make gains on the Turf remained in the hands of those who laid the odds. By the 1810 Derby, his betting records held at the Jockey Club show that he was by that time taking bets on a variety of horses from a fairly large number of men. [58]

He had become a well-known figure at the leading racecourses, notably at Newmarket where several of the largest stables were placed. His sources of information about horses and betting were second to none and he was making a good deal of money. 'He knew,' said William Day, 'how to worship the rising sun.' [59]

He was keeping his ear close to the ground and building up an impressive number of contacts with owners, trainers, jockeys, stable lads, indeed anyone who might know something which could be useful to him. He was also very aware that running a book was a dog eat dog world and that he needed to tread carefully and keep his wits about him, for 'there were other men in the business to watch: odd things were always happening and too much money against a horse from certain quarters was a thing to report'. [60]

He set to work to see if those wealthy patrons of his when he was a prize fighter could be persuaded to trust him to handle their betting transactions for them – in other words act as a go-between who could place large bets or commissions on their behalf. He knew too that it was a service that appealed particularly to the bigger gamblers and owners of the time who wished, for whatever reasons, to obscure a particularly sensitive piece of information, such as the form of a particular horse in training or its health. It was a role made for Gully and he set about exploiting the idea.

---

58   Foulkes, N. *Gentlemen and Blackguards.* p. 55
59   Blyth, Henry. *Hell and Hazard.* p.136
60   Darwin, B. *John Gully and his Times.* p.71

Commissioner

In a remarkably short period of time Gully succeeded in forming a group of wealthy men who were prepared to trust him with their commissions on a regular basis. This was a responsible but potentially lucrative position to hold. Once he had the agreement of a patron, he would spread the money around at his own discretion among other bookmakers, to ensure that he was getting the best price available, and to hedge the risk when necessary.

The recognised remuneration for commission business was around five per cent of the winnings though could be much more for a successful betting coup. His loyal patron from the boxing world, Colonel Mellish, was one of the first to use Gully for his commissions, and was soon followed by other heavy plungers (heavy bettors) and admirers of Gully such as Lord Abingdon, the Duke of Queensberry, and Lord Foley.

Gully was always helpful and respectful in his manner, and his clients appreciated the knowledge of horses, trainers and jockeys he had acquired and his judgement. They knew, too, that a man of Gully's determination could be relied upon to ensure that when they won their bets, the losers always paid up, and promptly. His reputation as a first-class commissioner gradually extended to the highest in the land and he began also to receive commissions from Lord George Bentinck, and the Duke of Clarence. (The Duke, later William IV, kept several racehorses and loved the sport, but seems to have had rather limited knowledge of their capability. When his trainer asked him what he should send down to run at Ascot for some big races, our sailor King replied, 'Why the whole squad, first-rates and gunboats; some of them, I suppose, must win.'). [61]

Becoming a successful betting commissioner had other important advantages for Gully himself. First and foremost, working with the big racehorse owners gave him access to

---

61   Longrigg, R. *The History of Horse Racing*. p.116

privileged information that could be used for his own benefit and there seems little doubt that he made good use of it. His less fortunate brethren of the Ring were forced to 'carry on their betting work pretty much in the dark'. [62]

Provided that he always put his employers' interests first, and his integrity could be relied upon, he saw no reason why he should not make some money out of such knowledge. Knowing that a particular horse had a good chance of winning made it possible for him to run a book of his own and to take bets in confidence against other horses in the field. A further advantage would not have escaped him, namely a social one. He was now mixing with leading members of the aristocracy and upper class and the trust they placed in him would have boosted his status in the social hierarchy.

Gully's betting books indicate that by 1825 the number of occasions he had laid bets on horses was reaching several thousand with often dozens of bets placed on just one race. The list of prominent heavy gamblers that he dealt with during this period is stunning, and none more so than the remarkable plunger George Payne, known as the King of Gamblers, and said to have gambled his way through three fortunes.

A man of considerable ability, Payne preferred to spend his life in pursuit of pleasure, especially hunting, horse racing and gambling. He would, he said, sooner be a Derby winner than become Prime Minister. However, his judgement was poor, and he was known to back a dozen or two horses in one race and still miss the winner!

Racehorse Owner

In a relatively short time Gully was doing well enough from bookmaking to fulfil one of his ambitions – to buy a racehorse of his own. Cardenio, a three-year-old, was the name of the horse. Racehorse owners mostly came from wealthy aristocrats

---

62   Curzon, L. *A Mirror of the Turf.* p.144

and land-owners and very few from working class backgrounds like Gully, so it signified another step up for him on the social scale. Still, he would have known that owning was an expensive and risky business.

The chances of winning a big prize were very remote. The costs of stabling, training and jockeys could be substantial. But he trusted his gambling instincts, and he seems to have been confident that with a bit of luck he could succeed as an owner. Anyone buying a racing horse – from kings and princes, to optimists or crooks – has visions of winning the Derby, and Gully would have been no more immune from that dream than anyone else. It would later become a prime obsession of his.

Cardenio ran for the first time for Gully at Chelmsford in 1812. He knew enough about horses to recognise that the horse was no great shakes as a racer and he made only a modest bet on it. Although it did not win, the new owner was pleased when it passed the winning post in a respectable position in the middle of the field.

The Death of His First Wife

In the autumn of 1822 Gully's personal life suffered badly. Mary had given birth to their 12th child, whom they named John. Unfortunately both mother and baby son died shortly afterwards. She was just 42 years old. It would have been a distressing time for John. He felt her loss badly. He was left a widower at a very busy stage of his racing career and with the added responsibilities of bringing up his growing family now placed on his shoulders. Perhaps this contributed to the impression some had that he had become a rather silent and taciturn man. On the other hand, Mary's death might just have strengthened his resolve to succeed in life.

Shortly after Mary had died, Gully was offered the chance of buying a large property near Newmarket – Upper Hare Park

– from Lord Rivers who was an enthusiastic admirer of Gully's success as a boxer. Gully was well aware of the fact that any rising gentleman in Regency England needed his own residence and estate. Upper Hare Park was just what he aspired to. It needed some decoration but was a sound and spacious residence well fitted for a gentleman with a large family. Moreover there were several acres of land to go with it which could be farmed, and at around £10,000, it was reasonably priced.

Gully continued to purchase more horses – Rigmarole, Tyke, Florentine, Hokee Pokee and Old England, to name but some. However, despite his efforts he was not yet able to get hold of a really first-class one. He kept a close eye on the racing world throughout the country and it was about this time his connection with the north of England began. He formed a close friendship with Richard Watt, a Yorkshire squire who was a prominent horse owner and trainer with a fine stud at the Bishop Burton Estate in the East Riding. As a commissioner, Gully began to make wagers regularly for Watt, and had some success himself from betting on the squire's horses. [63]

Gully retained an interest in the boxing scene but was now rarely seen at the ringside. He kept in touch with his former friends like Tom Cribb, but most of his old acquaintances were beginning to be left behind as he moved up the social scale. He was now spending much more of his time with highly respected sporting personages of the day like Lord Foley, Sir Tatton Sykes, Colonel Mellish and Squire Osbaldeston. He dressed in the fashionable clothes of the gentlemen of the time and was more likely to be addressed now as John Gully Esquire – a title used to denote someone with substantial wealth and position – rather than John Gully, the bruiser from Bristol.

Skulduggery

Gully's success in cornering several of the more lucrative

---

63   Darwin, B. *John Gully and his Times*. p. 74

betting commissions, plus the large amount of money he was clearly making, inevitably attracted attention and resentment in some quarters. His dealings became the subject of much rumour and adverse publicity. Much of it was derogatory, based around what was said to be his crooked and ruthless ways. There was particular concern about what was seen as the shady intelligence network which Gully had assiduously set up within the racing community.

This was bringing him a constant stream of up-to-date information from trainers, jockeys, touts and stable boys on how horses were faring in training and their prospects. In an age when there was not yet any system of mass communication or telegraph, having ready access to reliable inside information was very valuable indeed, and could be fairly easily exploited to make money or to minimise a loss.

There was a particularly insidious practice or betting coup (a successful betting move) requiring inside knowledge and which Gully and his associates were heavily criticised for making extensive use of. This was the practice of taking bets or laying them against what were termed dead 'uns – a horse which they knew full well would not run because it was unfit, gone lame or perhaps had even died! Consequently the punters had no chance of winning, and as was the rule in those days, anyone who had backed the horse beforehand would still have to pay up on their bet.

Just how much Gully involved himself in such a practice is difficult to know, though contemporary reports suggest it was highly likely. It was strongly held that for Harry Hill, who became one of Gully's closest confederates, it was the chief source of his own financial gains during his career.

The degree to which Gully was guilty of corrupt practices has often been discussed. Some contemporary and well-placed observers certainly believed so and thought very poorly of him. Charles Greville, a well-known racehorse owner and something of a literary figure, in his famous diaries accused Gully of creating in the 1820s, 'a system of corruption of trainers, jockeys and boys which put the secrets of Newmarket at his disposal and in a few years made him rich'. [64]

Greville later modified his opinion, and his testy comments on people need to be taken with a pinch of salt. His contemporary Benjamin Disraeli thought him to be the vainest man he had ever met. And then there was William Day, a prominent trainer of the time but no friend of Gully, who commented in his reminiscences, 'I don't think Mr Gully would stand very high in the esteem of his countrymen.' [65]

A modern historian of the Turf, Roger Longrigg, denounced Gully as the most evil man to be involved in horse racing in the 1800s. He accused Gully, together with his betting partners Ridsdale and Hill, of winning money through methods which were 'as crooked as they could be', and said that their principal technique was to bribe jockeys. [66]

On the other hand, it has to be remembered that by the standards of the day Gully's betting practices were far from unusual. Trickery, bribery and double-dealing were rampant, and Gully could not afford to be over-scrupulous on how he made his money. Even among respectable men, cheating at sports was to a degree acceptable and quite common. Paragons of the Turf such as Lord George Bentinck, a man who more than anyone was responsible for cleaning up the worst excesses of the racing world, was not averse to stooping low to score financially at the expense of others. [67]

In fact Gully's character and the way he went about his business were often highly praised. Thormanby, in his monumental *Kings of the Turf*, devoted a chapter to Gully, and

---

64   Greville, C.F. *The Diaries of Charles Greville.* ed. Pearce. p.110

65   Day, W. *Reminiscences of the Turf.* p.71

66   Longrigg, R. p.118

67   Seth-Smith, M. *Lord Paramount of the Turf.* p.69

described his career on the Turf as, 'a distinctly honourable one', and as far as he knew, 'he was never accused or even suspected of anything approaching foul play, but came out of every transaction in which he was engaged with clean hands.' [68]

Another reputable contemporary, Sylvanus, while admitting that he was not competent to comment on the ways Gully made money, thought he was a man, 'justly esteemed, having raised himself from the lowest paths of life… to a position of intimacy amongst gentlemen.' [69]

Pierce Egan described him as someone who, 'With a knowledge of the world he unites the manners of a well-bred man. Unassuming and intelligent upon all occasions, this conduct has gained him respect and attention in the circles in which he moves, and which are by no means of an inferior class. Thus proving that all pugilists are not excluded from polite society.' [70] Another person who formed a high opinion of Gully was the eminent essayist and critic William Hazlitt.

Several racing gentlemen were also impressed with Gully's open and honest manner compared with the sly and furtive ways of some of the other bookies. He was moreover always punctilious in paying off his gambling debts. As one contemporary said, 'It was not in the nature of Mr Gully to see a creditor near him without paying.' [71]

There was, however, one man who harboured no doubts that John Gully was as crooked as they come, and that was his arch rival, the infamous William Crockford. The rivalry between the two men became one of the most talked about affairs in the racing world of the time.

---

68   Thormanby, *Famous Racing Men*. p.32
69   Sylvanus. p.91.
70   Pierce Egan. *Boxiana*. p.186
71   Sylvanus. *Bye Lanes*. p.307

8

William Crockford

'Old Crocky, the father of hell and
hazard – ye fiends! What a title!'

WILLIAM Crockford had a career almost as remarkable as John Gully's. He was said by Roger Longrigg to be 'the second most evil man on the 19th -century turf'. [72] Longrigg seems to have regarded John Gully as the first! Born in 1775 within the sound of Bow Bells at Temple Bar in London, Crockford was a fishmonger's son. He grew up amid acute poverty in the slums near the stinking, dung-congested and dangerous River Thames. He was the founder of Crockford's in 1828 which became the most famous of all Regency gambling clubs. When he died aged nearly 70, he was one of the wealthiest men in England with a fortune worth in today's money of some £95m.

The Gambler

Crockford had a natural instinct for gambling. He was bold but not rash, and learned from an early age to bet when the odds

---

72 Longrigg, R. *The History of Horse Racing*. p.118

were in his favour and not when they were against him. His talent for numbers and the rapid calculation of betting odds soon freed him from a lifetime of gutting, scaling and selling fish. By the late 1790s he had become a professional gambler, well known at the races and around the boxing rings and a habitué of London's mainly low-class small-time gambling clubs known as silver hells, where the patrons could risk their shillings and half-crowns.

It took time for Crockford to rise above what was a corrupt and viciously competitive environment. But by the early 1800s he had accumulated sufficient capital to move to the more fashionable surroundings in London where he ran gambling houses at various addresses. It has to be acknowledged that Crockford had considerable vision, as well as courage, which enabled him to exploit the gambling fever that swept the Regency world. He soon recognised that one of the best ways to persuade the members of the rich and extravagant upper classes of the day to gamble with him was to create an environment in which even the most genteel aristocrat might feel at home.

Crockford's

In 1828 he took the bold decision to concentrate his gambling activities in an impressive building at the top of St James's Street in the West End of London. It was there that he created what became the greatest and most exclusive gentlemen's club in Europe, where all the rich and famous could meet and not only gamble but also enjoy free of charge the best food and the finest wines, and meet their friends.

When it opened in 1828 the newspapers were lavish with praise, and the memories of the time are full of references to Crockford's foresight in spotting the need for a club the like of which had not been seen elsewhere before. Despite Crockford's uncouth appearance and unpolished manners, it soon became immensely popular among the upper classes. At its peak it had over 800 members and included virtually all the celebrities and wealthy men of England. Even the prudent Duke of Wellington, who gambled only a little, could not resist the fascination of Crockford's, and became the first chair of its management committee (unlike another member, Field Marshal Blücher, who repeatedly lost everything he had at play).

Yet of course amid all the free food and wine, music and dancing, the sole purpose of the club was concentrated on the objective of fleecing the dissolute and rich at the gambling tables. The dice game, Hazard, was the most popular gambling game and played for very high stakes. It was said, 'The rattle of the dice was heard morning, noon, and night, thousands of pounds changing hands as if they were so many halfpence.' [73]

For many years there seemed to be no limit to Crockford's success and he eventually retired in 1840 with a fortune estimated to be around £1.2m, having won the whole of the ready money of the then existing generation. [74] As another contemporary dramatically put it, 'He retired much as an Indian chief retires from a hunting country when there is not game enough left for his tribe.' [75]

The following account demonstrates how Crockford, with a little help from one of his accomplices, went about drawing a gullible patron into his net:

'One night in June last, Lord Ashgrove lost £4,000 which he observed to the Earl of Linkwood, was the last farthing of ready cash at his command. The noble lord, however, had undeniable prospective resources. "Excuse me, my lud," said Crockford, making a very clumsy bow, "did I hear you say as you had no more ready money? My lud, th'ere is the ban' [pointing at the bank]; if your ludship wishes it, £1,000 or £2,000 is at your ludship's service."

73 Curzon, L. *A Mirror of the Turf*. p.267

74 William Crockford. wikipedia

75 Timbs, John. *Club Life of London*. p.241

'"Really, Mr Crockford, you are very obliging; but I don't think I shall play any more tonight." "Ashgrove," said Count Whiskeroo. "Ashgrove, do accept Mr Crockford's liberal offer of the £2,000, perhaps you may win all you have lost back."

'"Nothing, I assure your ludship, vill give me greater pleasure than to give you the money," said Crockford.

'"Well, let me have £2,000."

'Crockford dipped his fingers into the bank, took out £2,000 and handed it to his Lordship. "Per'aps your Ludship would obleege me with an IOU and pay the amount at your convenians."

'"I shall be able to pay the amount in a couple of months," said his Lordship, handing the fishmonger the IOU.

'"Your Ludship's werry kind – weery."

'Lord Ashgrove resumed the game. In an hour and a half he was again penniless.' [76]

The early 1800s saw Crockford spreading his gambling interests from the gambling tables in London to the Turf. He went about it in his typically resourceful and ambitious way. He moved to Newmarket where the best pickings could be made, and was soon mixing freely there with some of the leading blackleg bookmakers of the day such as Crutch Robinson, Harry Hill and Jem Bland.

He opened a gambling club in Newmarket at Rothsay House, and there he operated nightly both as a banker and bookmaker when the town's races were in progress. He bought an imposing house in the Newmarket High Street and a large farm on the east of the town. To complete his status as a proper Newmarket man, he began to buy racehorses in 1810, as well as breeding them at his stud farm.

Rivalry

It was inevitable that in a little while he would come up against John Gully, who was establishing his own position as a leading

---

76 *The American Quarterly Review.* Vol. 21, 1837 p.245

bookmaker and a man of substance in the town. He was a rival Crockford was not going to ignore. When the paths of the two men crossed, they took an instant dislike to one another and from then onwards they were to fight many a battle on the Turf. Gully looked down with disdain at the gross and scheming ex-fishmonger and his ostentatious ways, while Crockford sneered openly at Gully's lofty attitude and how he basked in the friendship and esteem of the upper classes. He was sure that beneath it all, Gully was just as cunning and devious as any other rogue. What was doubly galling to Crockford was that when the two crossed swords, it was usually himself who came out on the losing side.

On the face of it there are some striking similarities between their lives and character. Both were ambitious men who were determined to become successful and wealthy. Both were very clever bookmakers, with the ability to calculate quickly and more accurately than most of their rivals. Nor were they quite the fiends that some writers have described them. Both enjoyed horse racing and wanted to write their names into the history of the Turf by owning the best of horses and winning famous races. During his racing career Crockford invested in a large string of horses but they were never very successful, unlike Gully who was careful in his choice of horses.

Yet in many ways, however, the contrasts could not be sharper. For a start, their appearance was very different. Whereas Gully impressed with his smart clothes, upright bearing and honest face, Crockford could have hardly looked more disreputable – a thick-set man with a coarse florid face and massive bulbous nose, shifty look and hideous laugh. A contemporary was struck by his grotesque appearance, 'Old Crocky, the father of hell and hazard – ye fiends! What a title!... His cheeks appeared whitened and flabby through constant night-work. His hands were entirely without knuckles, soft as raw veal, and as white as paper, while his large flexible mouth stuffed with dead men's bones – teeth being all false, and visibly socketed with darling metal.' [77]

By nature cunning and devious, Crockford was outwardly servile and humble especially in the presence of the rich, but ever ready to plot their downfall. Gully projected a very different image, always polite, respectful and straightforward, a former boxing champion of England, and overall a chivalrous man that could be trusted.

The rivalry between the two men simmered for some years but erupted in the 1819 Derby at Epsom. Sultan, a fine and powerful bay horse that later became the champion sire in England during the mid-1830s, had been bred by Crockford and was by far the best horse he had so far owned. His main rival was a colt named Tiresias, owned by the Duke of Portland who was one of the most popular and respected racehorse owners of the time.

The betting was very heavy on the two contenders with Crockford backing his horse to win and Gully laying against a win for Sultan. Unusually for the two men, their stakes seem to have been guided more by the prejudice held against one another than from a shrewd judgement of racing performance. Crockford assumed that Tiresias would be no match for Sultan, while Gully, who at the time had little experience of the Epsom race, convinced himself that Tiresias would win. [78]

In a field of 16 runners, Tiresias started the 5/2 favourite for the Derby ahead of Sultan at 3/1, with 7/1 laid against the rest of the field. The race followed the course predicted by the betting. Ridden by the experienced jockey Bill Clift, Tiresias took the lead from the start and held on in the straight to win by a neck from Sultan, though others claim the victory was relatively easy. Gully could scarcely disguise his delight that

---

77   Sylvanus. *Bye Lanes*. p.62

78   Blyth, H. *Hell and Hazard*. p.77

the Duke's horse had won, while Crockford cursed his luck, his trainer, and especially his jockey for not making his challenge sooner.

At the time the Derby was still the preserve of the aristocracy and landed gentlemen. They too were happy that the Duke of Portland, the very best type of owner had won. They had seen off the challenge from nobodies like William Crockford, with his bags of money but no breeding or honesty. A Duke's horse had triumphed over that of a fishmonger. But it had been a very narrow victory and the future prospects of the Derby looked ominous. It would not be long before other dubious characters and upstarts, and even foreigners, would lay claim to England's premier Classic.

Crockford had to lick his wounds but drew some comfort from the fact his horse Sultan had also been entered later in the same season for the St Leger, a Classic race with a reputation almost as high as the Derby. This time Tiresias was not a runner, so the chances of Sultan winning looked very good and it was one of the favourites in the betting. In the weeks before the race Crockford once again backed Sultan heavily, while Gully bet against it.

However, this time Gully was basing his bets on hard information rather than emotion. His network of insiders and informers was telling him that the strain of preparing for another strenuous race had taken its toll on Sultan. Sure enough on the eve of the race, the horse broke down in his final gallop and had to be scratched from the race. As it happened both Gully and Crockford were still in London some 160 miles away and messages were sent to both men by post-chaise bearing the news.

However, the information reached Gully faster and for a few hours he continued to lay very generous odds against Sultan winning, knowing full well the horse would not run. Crockford, still blissfully unaware of what had happened, accepted those odds and continued to bet heavily on his horse. Much to his dismay, very soon after he learned that he had been outwitted by Gully and had lost a lot of his money in the process.

Gully had clearly behaved in an underhand and deceitful way, his only excuse being that he had simply acted in a way typical of the practice of the day. As for Crockford he had been caught with a dose of his own medicine and his hatred of Gully and his tricky ways intensified. The rivalry between the two men smouldered on for the next decade, both probably accepting that an open breach was not in either of their interests.

They were, after all, both professional bookmakers with an eye to maximising their income, and recognised that occasions could arise when they might well be useful to each other. Nonetheless, at the St Leger of 1827 Crockford at last seized upon a good opportunity to get his own back on his rival.

Revenge

Gully had done so well financially out of bookmaking and the commissions he held with wealthy men that he was now in a position to purchase a first-class racehorse. He bought in 1827 from Lord Jersey a horse called Mameluke for a fee of 4,000 guineas. The price was a very large one for those days but there was no doubt that Mameluke was a very good horse and had triumphed in the Derby earlier in the year. This purchase led to one of the biggest disasters in John Gully's racing career and came very close to ruining him.

Gully's prime aim at the time was to win the St Leger with his new horse. He made the purchase on the understanding that the notice of the sale would not be made known for 24 hours as he was anxious to wager on it at the best odds possible before news of the sale reached the betting Ring. Given his successful reputation as a betting man, he was only too aware that the odds would dip as soon as news of his purchase got out. The ploy worked, and Gully duly bet £1,000 on Mameluke to win at odds of 10/1. He reportedly stood to make more than £40,000 if the colt won.

Once the betting was over, Gully then revealed he was the new owner of Mameluke. Crockford was convinced that he had again been somehow duped by Gully and lost no time in planning his revenge. First, he used his contacts to find out just how good Mameluke was and his prospects of winning the race. Once he had learned that Mameluke was indeed outstanding and virtually a certainty to win the St Leger, he was determined to find some way to stop the horse winning the race. There was always the option of nobbling the horse in some way, but Gully would be bound to make sure that Mameluke was very closely guarded, and besides Crockford preferred to employ a more subtle method which could not possibly incriminate him.

It was well known in racing circles that Mameluke had one particular weakness which Crockford and his associates seized upon to exploit. The stallion was a highly temperamental thoroughbred and very easily upset. He could be put off his race if he were badly jostled at the start by other horses and their jockeys, and subjected to delays. And all that could be done in the open and seemingly above board. Crockford set to work. He first made it his business to get well acquainted with the starter of the race. Then he proceeded to buy off the owners of some of the horses with no real chance in the race, and their jockeys, with the promise they would be amply rewarded if their mounts were to prove unmanageable at the start, would agitate Mameluke and delay the off.

The plan worked well. Gully had taken great care to see that Mameluke was in prime condition and had not been interfered with in any way. He was somewhat surprised to see so many horses entered for the St Leger some of which had been barely broken in and with very little chance of winning, but he seems to have suspected nothing.

Mameluke arrived safely at the start and the normal procedure was for the jockeys to walk their mounts round slowly before being called by the starter to line up for the start. But this time things were completely different. A few of the jockeys were not even properly dressed for the race and their half-trained and barely broken mounts were rearing and pawing in the air. It was pretty obvious that some horses had been sent to the post with instructions to their jockeys never to start if Mameluke was in a position ready to go.

In accordance with their orders, so the story goes, the jockeys resisted every attempt to get off when Mameluke was in front of them. At last the Derby winner became so fretful and fractious that he would scarcely go near the starting flag. There were at least seven false starts before the race began. Seizing an unhappy moment when Sam Chifney Jnr (Mameluke's jockey) was turning his horse's head round and well to the rear, the starter dropped his flag and dispatched the field. Yet so great was Mameluke's speed that he made his way through all the horses, and in the final run-in he was beaten only by half a length by a horse called Matilda.

Gully watched from the grandstand with a glum face as the drama unfolded. The judges' verdict was not open to doubt – Matilda had won the St Leger. Gully knew he had been cheated and who was behind it. Not only had Crockford bribed the other owners and jockeys but also the starter, a Mr Lockwood (there was later an investigation into the scandalous behaviour of the starter and it was the last race that particular individual officiated in).

Gully paid his losses to Crockford without any comment but he was a very angry man. In all he had lost nearly £50,000, an enormous sum equivalent to well over £4m in today's prices, and which must have very nearly broken Gully. A family legend was that Gully had been helped out by a friend, Thomas Pedley, who had been left a small fortune by his father. [79] (Pedley later became his son-in-law and a racing partner of Gully.)

Whatever the truth of the matter, Gully never thought of leaving Tattersall's on Settling Day until all his debts had been honoured. He was said, when someone asked, 'Is it convenient for you to settle?' to have replied haughtily, 'It is always convenient, but it is not always pleasant.' [80]

So convinced was Gully of the superiority of his horse Mameluke over Matilda that he challenged Mr Petre the owner of Matilda to a match offering him a 7lb advantage in weight. However, Matilda's trainer, John Scott, would not hear of it and advised Mr Petre in strong terms that he had won the St Leger by a fluke, to pocket the £15,000 he had won, and thank his good fortune for what had happened.

Gully received a lot of credit for the gentlemanly way he had reacted to being cheated at the St Leger but he was never going to forget what had happened and resolved one day to have his revenge. Crockford, meanwhile, had done very well out of the whole affair and the money was put to good use in furnishing his magnificent new gambling club in the West End. He would have known that his arch enemy was not a man to let matters rest, and so it later proved.

The two men were never reconciled. Their bitter rivalry rumbled on for several years and was last fought out at the infamous Running Rein Derby of 1844 just three days before Crockford died.

There was an interesting sequel to the Mameluke saga. In 1829 Gully rather rashly sold the horse to a Mr Theobald of Stockwell, a fine old English sportsman whose ambition was to have the best of everything. Gully immediately repented of what he had done. Apparently Gully's new wife, Mary Lacey,

---

79 Darwin, B. *John Gully and His Times*. p.90
80 Blyth, H. *Hell & Hazard*. p.99

was very upset to see the horse go without her consent. Gully tried all in his power to get the horse back, even to the extent of letting the new owner have a blank cheque, telling him to complete it for any sum in reason. But Mr Theobald – Old Leather Boot, as he was called – refused to budge, replying, 'Then you must make up your tiff without the horse for no money will induce me to part with him.'

So the horse remained for several years, the pride of the Stockwell stud, until he was shipped to an American breeder in the United States.

9

Bob Ridsdale

*'How much they won no two
chroniclers seem to agree.'*

IN the late 1820s a shudder of apprehension swept through
the racing fraternity when they heard that two of the most
formidable and prosperous of all the legs – John Gully and
Robert Ridsdale – had agreed to form a betting partnership.
They had good reason, for over the next few years the two
men pulled off a number of betting coups which astonished
the betting world.

Robert Ridsdale

At first sight the partnership seemed an unlikely one since the
pair had clashed in the past and were very different characters.
Gully came across as a strong, quiet, resolute man, highly
respected and trusted, but with no great subtlety or finesse,
whereas Ridsdale was just the opposite, and had earned a
reputation as the cleverest villain on Newmarket Heath (there
was a strong suspicion that Ridsdale had been implicated in the
Mameluke scandal and Gully would have known about that).

He had begun his career as a groom to the immensely rich John Lambton, afterwards the first Earl of Durham. A quick learner, he soon built up a considerable knowledge of horse racing especially in the north of England. With his good looks, pleasant manner and quick wit, he quickly stood out among the other legs. Like Gully, he had a reputation for always being punctual in his payments whatever his losses, and obtained some lucrative commissions from some of the big plungers.

In practice however it turned out initially to be the ideal partnership. They may not have got on too well with one another but they respected each other's abilities, and both enjoyed playing the part of a country gentleman. They also had one critical common interest – to make as much money as they could, and if that required some devious and questionable practices, so be it.

The heavy losses that Gully had taken at the 1827 St Leger had taught him an important lesson – clever as he was, he still needed a betting partner with expertise, skills and experience that would complement his own. Gully knew that no man was better equipped than Robert Ridsdale for flattering and managing trainers and jockeys for their own and other people's advantage. George Payne, who lost a good deal of money to Ridsdale over the years, always declared that Ridsdale was 'the most dexterous and dangerous manipulator of jockeys and trainers that he had ever encountered'. [81]

Ridsdale's machinations however were not always successful and in 1824 he had found himself the principal agent in a notable racing scandal involving a muscular bay horse named Jerry. The horse was the property of a Richard Gascoigne whose very experienced trainer, James Croft, reckoned it was a near certainty that Jerry would win the St Leger of that year.

The horse was in fine condition and there was plenty of money behind him at the odds of 5/2. Oddly, however, as much

81   Darwin, B. *John Gully and His Times*. p.94

as Jerry was backed, the odds against suddenly lengthened, and the betting Ring, including Ridsdale and Gully, began to wager persistently against the horse. Neither the owner nor his trainer could discover any cause for the change. Jerry was as well as ever and was most carefully watched and guarded.

There was something very suspicious going on, and the trainer began to suspect that it was the jockey rather than the horse which had been got at. Harry Edwards was the jockey engaged to ride Jerry. Edwards had many virtues as a jockey but there was considerable doubt about some of his other qualities. The popular view was that Edwards could not go straight, and given the chance he enjoyed 'doing a bit on the quiet on his own account, and putting the double dodge on the swells'. [82]

A few days before the race the odds against Jerry winning had drifted out to 10/1 and to calm his nerves Croft took a walk one evening down Doncaster's Great North Road. As he paused to speak with the man at the turnpike, a post-chaise drove up and by the light from the windows of a roadside inn he saw that the occupants of the vehicle were Harry Edwards, very drunk, and Ridsdale. He hurried off to Mr Gascoigne and told him what he had seen. They agreed to keep the incident dark and not say a word to Edwards or anyone else. Fortunately, they had another good jockey ready at hand called Ben Smith, a man honest to the core and the 'most quiet simple-minded creature that ever trod Yorkshire ground'. [83]

Shortly before the race was to start, Edwards, dressed in Mr Gascoigne's colours, was preparing to mount Jerry, when James Croft tapped him on the shoulder and said, 'Not today Mr Edwards, thank you.' Whereupon, Ben Smith, dressed in Gascoigne's colours, quietly took his place, much to the consternation of punters in the Ring. The betting odds turned

82 Sylvanus. Quote in Darwin. *John Gully*. p.84
83 Darwin, B. *John Gully and his Times*. p.85

in a flash and were now all in favour of Jerry, who fully justified his backers by winning the St Leger from the other 22 runners.

Since Ridsdale had strongly advised his patrons to support other horses rather than Jerry in the race, some heavy losses had been incurred. Gully too had been caught out by the knavery. Although there is no evidence that he had anything to do with the plot, he knew that Ridsdale must be on to something and had advised his own clients accordingly.

As a result one of Gully's wealthiest and closest clients, George Payne, still only a lad of 20, was left with the prospect of having to find some £20,000 to £30,000. He bore that huge loss with the insouciance typical of the age amongst gentlemen, and when consoled by his friends, he replied, 'Oh! It's a pleasure to lose, by Jove!'

Gully, rarely sentimental and who had also lost badly on the race, was struck by Payne's courage and cheerful nature. The following day he met Payne behind the stand and told him, 'I am very sorry, Mr Payne, for what has occurred, but we were entirely deceived. I heard from what I thought the best authority that Jerry was infirm and doing no work whatever.' But Payne replied, 'Jerry's owner and his owner's friends never ceased backing him, and his trainer gave them the most encouraging reports.'

'That is true,' said Gully, 'but I had the fullest reason to believe that Croft was having a race for himself. It was a trap laid for me, into which I fell, and unfortunately led you to follow me. Now, mark my words, if you will be guided by my advice, you will get all your money back this time next year.' Gully told him to back Memnon in the St Leger for the following year, which Payne did, so 'availed himself with the most satisfactory results'. [84]

The Jerry scandal had been a bad blow for Ridsdale. Nonetheless by 1830 in partnership with Gully he had

---

84 Thormanby. *Kings of the Turf.* p.107

recovered to become a wealthy man and was at the height of his personal popularity. He was a generous person and for all his poor background and shady dealings, he was acknowledged to have 'wonderful good taste, tact and sense of propriety'. [85]

His residence at Murton Hall in Yorkshire was relatively small but exquisitely furnished regardless of cost, and if you stayed there you could luxuriate in all the comforts and be treated like royalty. He was a big spender and fond of the fleshpots, and loved horses for their own sake. At one time it was said that he had as many as a hundred racehorses on his estate besides hunters and farm horses. He was also very fond of hunting. Everybody liked him. There might be a few disreputable tales about gallant Ridsdale but they could be easily forgiven.

The Partnership

The link-up between Gully and Ridsdale proved very successful. They had plenty of rich clients and they made some shrewd and clever gambles. 'How much they won no two chroniclers seem to agree, but it would have been a significant amount of money.' [86] An old stableman of the time wrote, 'When John Gully and his pal Ridsdale were a-carrying all before them, I can mind when pails of champagne wine were stood by the winners and stable boys turned up their noses at it. [The] Gentlemen would think nothing of giving me a sovereign for a-holding their hacks for 10 minutes.' [87]

It was joked, too, that when Gully and his friends descended on the Cheltenham racecourse, they so completely cleaned out the local betting Ring that they did not even think it worthwhile stopping for the second race day! One of the

---

85   Robert Ridsdale, *Licensed Victuallers' Gazette, Otago Witness*. 25 November 1887

86   Darwin, B. *John Gully and his Times*. p.108

87   Curzon, L. *A Mirror Of the Turf*. p.62

lesser legs was found later wandering moodily about the ring, and remarked to a sympathiser that he was looking for the few half-crowns which Gully had condescended to leave. [88]

Their network of racing informers was second to none. They paid handsomely for information, and were probably not above using a little bribery to grease the palms if necessary. When they stood cheek by jowl with each other in the grandstand at races the contrast was stark – Gully, in an open waistcoat and frock cloak, a somewhat crumpled diamond studded shirt and a not too scrupulously brushed hat, while his partner Ridsdale always dressed immaculately from the tips of his brilliantly polished boots to his shiny hat and in clothes, 'cut such as a duke might affect, but nothing more'. [89]

Gully was never going to try to make himself quite so agreeable with everyone as Ridsdale, and may even have been a little jealous and in awe of him. But for the moment differences could be put aside and they soon showed that they could work very successfully together for mutual advantage.

Although Gully had become a highly respected racehorse owner and had been successful in several minor races, he had never won any of the most important races, especially one of the Classics. His overriding ambition was to win the Derby – the Blue Ribbon of the Turf – and his partnership with Ridsdale was very much focused on that objective.

Their first serious attempt was made in the 1830 Derby when they entered their colt Little Red Rover in the race and backed him heavily. If the horse had carried off the race, it was reckoned that the pair would have won upwards of £80,000.

In a field of 23 horses the favourite in the Derby was Priam at odds of 4/1. He was ridden by the veteran jockey Sam Day.

---

88 The Druid. p.49

89 Robert Ridsdale. *Licensed Victuallers' Gazette. Otago Witness.* 25 November 1887

The race was run in heavy rain, but attracted the customary huge crowd. There was a suspicion that there was an attempt to unsettle Priam by a succession of false starts reminiscent of what had unsettled Mameluke at the St Leger in 1827, but Priam – a most docile and tractable colt – remained unruffled. In all there were 13 or 14 false starts before the race began an hour late and with Priam being left behind by the other runners. Day, however, quickly made up the ground and was in fifth place behind Little Red Rover as the horses approached the turn into the straight. He waited until the final furlong before taking Priam with a strong run into the lead and winning by two lengths from Little Red Rover.

Gully did not have to wait long to get over his disappointment. The 1832 season turned out to be a very successful one for the partnership when it won both the Derby and the St Leger. The winner of the Derby was St Giles, owned jointly by Gully and Ridsdale. Gully was delighted but the race was not free of controversy.

St Giles was a dark chestnut stallion bred by Mr Cattle, a farmer from Sheriff Hutton in Yorkshire. In fact little was known about the horse since it had been very lightly raced as a two-year-old and some suspicions emerged that its true form was being covered up. Gully also had another horse in the race, Margrave, a big, ugly looking, dark chestnut colt with lop ears and an unattractive head, but he raced with a fine sweeping action, and was generally held to be a much superior horse to St Giles. Although Ridsdale and Gully protested that St Giles was simply an unknown quantity, both of them had backed him very heavily, so much so that on the day of the race despite its modest form, St Giles was made favourite to win at odds of 3/1 in a field of 22 runners. Something strange clearly had been going on.

The race took place at Epsom on 7 June. After several false starts, another of Ridsdale's horses, Trustee, set a very strong pace with St Giles, ridden by Bill Scott, settling into third place. By halfway, many of the runners were struggling but St Giles was still going well and turned into the straight in second place. With two furlongs to go, Scott sent St Giles past Trustee and into the lead. He was never seriously challenged and won comfortably. Perion took second place, and Trustee and Margrave third and fourth respectively. Ridsdale, Gully, and their great rival Crockford, were reported to have taken a combined total of almost £100,000 (over £9m today) on the race, in addition to the £2,775 prize money. [90]

It was the manner of St Giles's victory, however, that confirmed suspicions. Gully's horse, Margrave, did not appear to have been given a hard race, and both the *Quarterly Review* and the *Sporting Review* expressed the opinion that he had been held back from winning on Gully's instructions as it was destined for the St Leger. It was widely believed that some of the runners had also been made safe, meaning that their jockeys or trainers had been bribed to ensure their horses did not win. An objection to St Giles's victory was made but the stewards overruled it. But the issue remained controversial and given his past misdemeanours the finger of suspicion pointed firmly at the ingenious Ridsdale as probably being the man behind it all, but no skulduggery was ever pinned upon him or in fact Gully.

The End of the Partnership

Gully had achieved his objective in becoming a Derby winner but the race effectively spelt the end of the partnership. A bitter dispute between the two men, triggered predictably over money, broke out on the Settling Day following the event. The quarrel arose out of the vast amount of money Ridsdale and Gully had won on the race, and how it should be divided up. Ridsdale had wagered a considerably higher amount on St

---

90 https://en.wikipedia.org/wiki/St._Giles_(horse)

Giles than Gully, and had won £40,000 to £50,000 exclusive of the stake money of £2,775.

Gully, although he had bet a lower amount, claimed he was entitled to about half of the winnings. Though on the face of it the balance of the argument seems to have been with Ridsdale, there was probably much more behind the dispute than is known. Consequently, Gully declared the partnership was ended. It was a bitter and acrimonious separation, especially as Ridsdale then took relish in spreading around the racing scene his own version of the story.

Meanwhile, the St Leger later in 1832 had worked out on the lines the partners had originally planned – Gully's horse Margrave was the winner, beating a large field comfortably. He seems to have derived more satisfaction from this victory than he had with his Derby success. With the betting odds on Margrave at 16/1 against, he appeared to have no chance and when his horse galloped past the winning post ahead of his rivals, Gully's tumultuous shout of 'I've won' could be heard two or three furlongs down the course.

However, the race intensified the dispute between Gully and Ridsdale. Since Margrave had run in Gully's name and colours, he had no hesitation in claiming the larger share of the winnings. This time it was Ridsdale's turn to protest vehemently, and he continued to spread scurrilous stories around Newmarket about what he claimed were his former partner's double-dealings. [91]

The row between the two men persisted and came to a dramatic climax in a personal encounter on the hunting field on a misty day in November 1833 when by chance the two men met. Gully accused Ridsdale of being behind all the rumours about the excessively large winnings Gully had made on their earlier races (accounts vary whether it was on the Derby or the St Leger though probably the latter) Ridsdale refused to

---

91   Blyth, H. *Hell and Hazard*. p.134

back down whereupon Gully in a fury thrashed him with his hunting crop 'with all the force that the arm of Gully could bestow'. [92]

Ridsdale promptly brought a legal action for assault against Gully which was heard at York before Mr Justice Taunton and a special jury.

In summing up the case, Justice Taunton said that the question for the jury should be the amount of the damages Mr Gully should pay to the plaintiff. He concluded that Mr Ridsdale had given no provocation, and the blow Gully had struck was altogether a wanton and uncalled for assault. He went on to say that, although the plaintiff had not received any injury, the jury had to consider what a person with the rank of a gentleman, in which social class both men were acknowledged to move, should receive for such an insult as that.

At the end of proceedings the jury took only ten minutes to reach their verdict and awarded the plaintiff £500 in damages. The bulk of the spectators in the crowded court were Yorkshire hunting men with whom Bobby Ridsdale was very popular, and the decision was met with so much approval, 'that they gave a rattling holloa, in which the learned brethren of the Bar and the eminent Judge himself were maliciously reported at the time to have cordially joined'. [93]

Although the court verdict was a triumph for Ridsdale, the break-up of his partnership with Gully signalled the former's downfall. Thereafter, he seems to have lost his touch. His speculations proved unfortunate and despite a few successes, he was losing large amounts of money in addition to his prodigious personal expenses running at some £10,000 a year.

His last throw was to come in the 1835 St Leger when he placed an enormous stake on Hornsea to win the race. It was a reasonable bet in so far as Hornsea was a good horse and at

92 Darwin. B. *John Gully and His Times*. p.188
93 Day,W. *Reminiscences*. p.623

odds of 2/1 was judged to be better than virtually all other horses in the field. The favourite, Queen of Trumps, had won the Oaks in a canter but had little other form to go on. Unfortunately for Ridsdale, although Hornsea briefly took the lead in the last quarter of a mile he was still beaten by the Queen by a length.

Ridsdale in fairness did what he could to meet his creditors but was forced to sell his home and all the pictures, his farm, his horses, and other belongings. His friends would have helped him if he would have let them, and even Gully is said to have been prepared to forget old scores and help him. But Ridsdale was a proud man and resolutely rejected all offers of help. He had one respite when he was able to share some of the winnings of his brother, William, who surprisingly won the Derby in 1839 at very good odds with a horse that Ridsdale had given him earlier.

However, his fortunes continued to decline. When he backed a horse it failed, and whenever he bet against one, it turned out to be a winner. He disappeared from his old haunts and no one knew what had become of him. He became a broken man, and eventually drifted back to the scene of his past glories, Newmarket.

One cold November morning in 1855 he was found dead by a stable lad in a loft over his master's stable. When searched, just three halfpence were found in the corner of one of his pockets. There was an inquest and Robert Ridsdale, aged 54, the man who had at one time, 'played with thousands as ordinary men play with shillings', was consigned to a pauper's grave. [94]

---

94 *Licensed Victuallers' Gazette. Otago Witness.* 25 November 1887

10

Member of Parliament

*'Some very bad characters,
however, have been returned;
among the worst Gully, at
Pontefract.'*

APART from his involvement in bare-knuckle fighting
and horse racing, another twist in the extraordinary
career of John Gully came on 10 December 1832
when he astonished his friends and enemies alike by taking his
seat in the first Reformed Parliament as the elected Member of
Parliament for the Pontefract constituency of the West Riding
of Yorkshire.

The Reform Act
Before the 1830s, British parliamentary elections were neither
representative nor balanced. The main purpose of the first
Reform Act of 1832 was to make parliamentary representation
more equal by transferring seats from the less densely inhabited
places (the rotten boroughs) controlled by the nobility and

gentry, to the fast-growing industrial towns like Birmingham, Leeds and Sheffield which had no representation.

Reformers had objected to rotten boroughs because the MPs who sat for them were accountable to the borough patron, often aristocratic, rather than to the electorate. The Act was by no means a revolutionary measure, nor 'the final solution of a great constitutional question', as Lord George Russell, one of the leading reformers, had put it. But both symbolically and physically, it spelt the beginning of big changes to Britain's electoral system.

The Act certainly changed the composition of the House of Commons. There were 510 so-called reformers – Whigs, radicals and the Irish members – compared with just 150 Tories. In came merchants, industrialists, entrepreneurs, shopkeepers, tenant farmers, radical journalists like William Cobbett, and much to everyone's surprise, a former butcher and prize fighter turned successful bookmaker and racehorse owner – John Gully.

The historic town of Pontefract can trace its representation back to the Model Parliament of 1295, and before the Reform Act was classed as a parliamentary borough returning two members, consisting only of the town of Pontefract. In fact Pontefract was no more than a pocket borough, where the Earl of Harewood had the effective power to choose one of its two MPs.

The 1832 Act extended the boundaries of the Pontefract borough to include neighbouring towns such as Knottingley, Monkhill and Ferrybridge.

The new constituency continued to send two members to the House of Commons and even with reform, the electorate was still a relatively narrow one confined mainly to the propertied middle class. Its expansion to the lower-middle and working classes, and the voting by secret ballot, were reforms which still lay in the future.

The Pontefract Election

Just why and how Gully decided to stand for election to Parliament is not clear and on the face of things it was an odd choice given that he was a very busy man and his racing career was flourishing.

He would have been aware of the additional honour and prestige which came with the position and that becoming a Member of Parliament would certainly confirm his status as a gentleman in the social hierarchy. It is unlikely, however, that he did it for sheer vanity. He was proud of his achievements, but he was not a conceited man, seeking fame for fame's sake. Nor was he particularly political.

Gully had progressive views and favoured improvements, but was hardly an 'ardent reformer and liberal subscriber for the advancement of the Cause', as Charles Greville described him after the election. [95]

He would have followed with concern the riots that had swept towns in England before 1832 when Parliament initially had decided against electoral reform. His former home town of Bristol was the scene of some of the bloodiest riots. Protesters had stoned the Mansion House, broken in and destroyed it. The Bristol gaol and Bishop's Palace were also set on fire. In total an estimated 70 people died in the violence.

His election probably arose more by chance than design. He was undoubtedly fortunate in being in the right place at the right time. The liberal reformers of Pontefract were desperate to have their interests in Parliament represented by a man of substance with good connections. Gully, they reckoned, as a famous sportsman and prosperous gentleman residing locally in a fine country seat at Ackworth Park, would be an ideal candidate. They decided to approach him with the offer of standing as one of their two candidates for Pontefract in the forthcoming 1832 election.

---

95   Darwin, B. *John Gully and his Times*. p.123

Gully seems to have been taken by surprise and his first reaction appears to have been negative. He explained that he supported their cause and appreciated the honour, but pointed to his limited knowledge of public affairs and to his poor education. Besides, he explained, he had little experience of public speaking and by temperament was a man of few words. Nonetheless, he was flattered that he had been asked and offered to do what he could to help their campaign.

True to form, once Gully became caught up in the fierce electioneering that preceded the 1832 election, his relish for a battle took over and he had a change of heart. He also took a particular dislike to the arrogant manners of the Tory candidate – Viscount Pollington, son of the Earl of Mexborough.

In a previous Parliament, Pollington had voted consistently against the passing of the Reform Bill. Significantly, he had also voted to end the grant to the important Roman Catholic Maynooth College in Ireland. That would have certainly rankled with Gully's new wife, Mary Lacey, who was a devout Catholic. Overall, Pollington was just the sort of man an old bruiser like Gully liked to put down and he now let it be known that he would be prepared to stand for Parliament after all.

On 3 November 1832, shortly before the election took place, the supporters from all the candidates met together at the Pontefract Town Hall to decide finally who should be the candidates of the forthcoming election. The meeting was apparently a very stormy one but the Liberal supporters at last agreed unanimously to approach Gully and formally offer him the honour of becoming their candidate.

This time Gully did not restrain himself and in a speech from the balcony of the Red Lion Inn in Pontefract, he gratefully accepted the offer and mounted a rousing attack on the opponents of reform. His Liberal supporters were delighted, and to celebrate his nomination decided that they would all march for Gully through Pontefract at 8am the following day. The march took a little time to assemble but by 10.30am 'they were in full march with colours flying and drums beating'. [96]

John must have been impressed by the demonstration of support and surely it would have triggered memories of the time over 20 years earlier when the Dunstable volunteers had similarly marched through their own town before his fight with Bob Gregson. Significantly, the march also showed the depth of support the citizens of Pontefract held for the Reform party, and consequently Viscount Pollington decided to beat a retreat and withdrew before the poll, leaving John Gully and another Liberal, the Hon. H. Stafford Jerningham, unopposed. The two men were duly elected by a show of hands to take up their seats in the new Parliament. Sir George Hayter's famous picture of the meeting of the First Reformed Parliament shows John Gully proudly occupying a prominent place on the government back benches

Like most elections of the time, the Pontefract poll was not without its controversy. Elections could be an expensive process and often open to corruption. Gully's opponents later accused him of spending his money profusely within the constituency, and that he had even ensured that free barrels of beer had been made available in the run-up to the election. Gully firmly denied the accusations and there is no firm evidence that any of his money was used in such ways to canvass support.

For a butcher's son and a former prize fighter to enter Parliament was truly a remarkable event and very probably without precedent (legend has it that Cardinal Wolsey was the son of a butcher but there is no evidence to bear that out and he was in fact the son of a prosperous merchant). Some might still sneer at Gully's background and despise the ways in which he had made his fortune, but the fact remains that John Gully Esquire, with only the most basic education, had

---

96   Ibid. p.125

risen to take a seat in what was, with the Lords, the highest legislative body in the land.

But by no means everyone was pleased to see Gully elected. Many were simply alarmed by the prospect of extending the franchise and the admission of people into the Commons without what they considered the appropriate knowledge and experience. Charles Greville, for example, was often friendly enough to Gully in public, but in private it was too often the opposite. Perhaps he showed his true feelings by writing in his diary, 'The borough elections are nearly over and have satisfied the Government. They do not seem to be bad on the whole…Some very bad characters, however, have been returned; among the worst…Gully, Pontefract.' [97]

And a writer of the time, James Smith, on learning of Gully's success, penned these few biting lines:

> You ask me the cause that made Pontefract sully
> Her fame by returning to Parliament Gully
> The etymological cause I suppose is
> His breaking the bridges of so many noses.

The name of Pontefract is derived from the Latin name for Broken Bridge.

The Commons

The Whig party under Lord Charles Grey, that had been elected to government in 1832, at first showed little interest in pressing for more radical reform. Gully was quite content to take his time to adjust to his new surroundings, quietly showing himself to be a loyal supporter of the government. He claimed that he was a democrat in the strictest sense and was an earnest supporter of the Bills for the abolition of slavery and for the relief of the Dissenters. [98] But by no stretch of the imagination

---

97   Greville, Charles. Quoted in Thormanby. *Kings of the Turf.* p.38
98   *Leeds Times.* 22 April 1837.

could John Gully be called a great Parliamentarian and showed no appetite for taking a leading role on any particular social or economic matter.

Hansard has no record of him actually making a speech in the House about anything of a political character. There is a story, but perhaps an unlikely one, that when he rose to make his maiden speech some wag called out 'time' and Gully replied that the honourable member should not act as the referee! But by all accounts he took the status of an MP seriously. He impressed with his calm and dignified manner. He was a popular member in the House and there were always plenty of sporting members who sought out his company, no doubt eager to learn at first hand more about his experiences in the prize ring and on the Turf.

A particular friend of Gully and family was the famous Irish politician Daniel O'Connell, nicknamed the 'Agitator'. Gully's daughters were being brought up as Catholics and O'Connell appears to have been at some time an admirer of his pretty young daughter, Mary Gully. O'Connell had always told her that she ought to become a nun, advice she seems to have heeded little since she married Thomas Pedley at the tender age of 17.

O'Connell as a young man loved to hunt on the high hills of Kerry and much enjoyed sports of a rough and tough character. On one occasion when he was on the way to the Commons to deliver a characteristic five-hour-long speech, he received a smart slap on the back. 'There you are, Dan O'Connell,' cried Gully with a laugh, 'going down cool and quiet to your work.' 'Yes,' replied O'Connell, and playing along with the humour of the situation, he threw himself into a boxer's stance to the great amusement of the crowd, and added, 'Tell me, Gully, is not that the way to do it?' [99]

---

[99]   Geoghegan, P.M. *Liberator Daniel O'Connell*. Quotation.

Gully also made a favourable impression on Charles Dickens, who described the new member for Pontefract in his Parliamentary Sketches in the following way, 'The quiet gentlemanly-looking man in the blue surtout, grey trousers, white neckerchief, and gloves, whose closely buttoned coat displays his manly figure and broad chest to great advantage, is a well-known character. He has fought a great many battles in his time, and conquered like the heroes of old, with no other arms than those the Gods gave him.' [100]

Speech

On 17 May 1836 Gully was roused to make at least one noteworthy speech. The occasion was a debate in the Commons on the alleged eviction of Roman Catholic tenants by Protestant landlords in the county of Carlow in south-east Ireland. Absentee landlords were common in Ireland and for many of them their primary focus was income rather than the conditions of their tenants. Some also calculated that they could get a higher income by turning their properties to pasture rather than continuing with the practice of collecting rents from tenant farmers. Evictions were the most common way of getting rid of unwanted tenants.

It was a cause that attracted Gully's sympathy and he would have listened carefully to the discussion. But he may not have been drawn into the debate if John Hardy, the Conservative member for Bradford, had not used the occasion to settle some old scores he had with O'Connell, the Irish member. Gully had little time for Hardy, and would have relished an opportunity to rally to the support of his friend, especially as O'Connell happened to be absent from the Chamber at the time and was not able to defend himself.

The dispute between Hardy and O'Connell goes back to the 1826 election for the old borough of Pontefract when

---

100 Dickens, C. Parliamentary Sketches by Boz

O'Connell had twice accused him of bribery at that event. At the time Hardy said nothing but he bided his time to take his revenge. Now the boot was on the other foot. O'Connell himself was involved in an allegation that he was willing to help a Catholic banker, Alexander Raphael, to run as a candidate for the Carlow seat, but required a sum of £2,000 in return. Party feeling ran high, and the Tory party accused O'Connell of corruption.

The affair reflected badly on O'Connell's reputation and dragged on for some time. The Tory press took the opportunity to brand the whole of Ireland as a place where every adventurer, provided he had a sufficient sum in hand was welcome, whether Christian, Heathen, Turk or Jew. A House of Commons Committee was eventually set up to look into the affair but was unable to find enough evidence to support the allegations and exonerated O'Connell from all charges of corruption.

However, Hardy was far from satisfied. He reminded the House that in 1833 he had brought in a Bill against bribery and corruption at elections, and while that Bill was still in progress through the House, he felt it was most extraordinary that allegations were still being made against him to the effect that he was an unfit person to bring such a Bill forward. He thanked the House for its indulgence in allowing him to enter upon a matter so deeply affecting his character, and concluded by expressing a hope that 'whatever steps the House should take…they would take care that justice was done not only in regard to Carlow, but to any other part of the country which might ever become the object of a similar investigation'. [101]

It was at that point when Gully rose to his feet to observe that it was very seldom that he claimed the indulgence of the House; but on the present occasion, after what had transpired, it was quite impossible for him to refrain from making a few

---

101 Hansard. 17 May 1836

observations. He said that he had distinctly heard on two occasions Mr O'Connell accusing Mr Hardy in the House of spending £7,041 on bribing electors in the borough of Pontefract to the amount of £23 for a single vote.

And yet the honourable and learned Member for Bradford had not given any explanation on either of those occasions. Gully went on to say that in the last three days one of his constituents had sent him a copy of a letter in which Hardy had stated clearly how much the constituent concerned would receive for his vote at the election. Hardy was enraged and demanded that the letter should be produced and read in Parliament. Gully replied that the letter was at home and promised that he would bring it down to the House the very next day.

However, there was a delay, either because Gully was unable to find the letter, or perhaps the man concerned was uncomfortable about the letter being read in Parliament. It was not until 22 June 1836 that Gully returned to the charge with the letter and read it out aloud to the House. The letter written by Hardy in March 1834 left no doubt that he had indeed been guilty of paying head money to those who had voted for him, though he argued, 'much against my conscience'. In one way or another, he admitted that had paid more than £5,000 in connection with the election. [102]

The disclosure of the letter caused uproar in the House and a long and angry debate took place. But the whole issue was eventually hushed up, as there were very few members of a reformed Commons who wished to see such a distasteful subject being aired for too long publicly. It did, however, constitute a minor triumph for Gully and during the whole course of the debate he always remained calm and dignified. At one point he was challenged by Hardy as to whether he himself had ever paid head money, in other words bribes.

---

102 Darwin, B. *John Gully and his Times*. pp.129/130

Gully replied, 'He would answer the honourable and learned gentleman that if he had paid head money and had afterwards declared that he never had been guilty of bribery in any shape whatever, he should consider himself unworthy of a seat in that House.' [103] It was a retort that completely floored Hardy, and Gully had 'metaphorically turned a cheerful somersault out of the ring and Mr Hardy lay prone'. [104]

Re-Election

When another general election was called in 1835 Gully agreed to stand again as the Liberal candidate for his constituency. Polling took place in January and February and the results saw Robert Peel's Conservatives make large gains though the Whigs maintained a big majority. This time there was an actual contest between the two political parties in Pontefract for the two parliamentary seats, and Gully was elected together with his rival, the Conservative candidate Viscount Pollington. When, however, Parliament was dissolved just two years later on the death of King William IV, Gully decided that he would not stand again.

His supporters tried to persuade him to change his mind but to no avail. He claimed he did not like the late hours which had proved injurious to his health. It is probable that he had found the parliamentary duties, in addition to his horse racing and business commitments in the north, notably his investments in the Durham coal mines, were simply taking up too much of his time and energy.

When he notified his intention of retiring, his supporters in Knottingley, part of the Pontefract constituency, organised a sumptuous dinner for him at the Swan Inn as 'a token of their admiration of his parliamentary conduct, and of gratitude for his services'. The chairman of the dinner somewhat effusively

---

103 Hansard Debate on Pontefract Election. 22 June 1836
104 Darwin, B. *John Gully and his Times*. p.130

praised Gully for his parliamentary record and 'defied anyone to point out a single vote opposed to the rights and liberties of Englishmen, or injustice to the institutions of the country'.

In his reply, Gully responded in kind, and emphasised his democratic principles, roundly declaring, 'It had been my sincere desire to see the conditions of the poor ameliorated – to extend to all classes, equal laws and equal privileges, to reduce the national expenditure and to allow every man to worship God according to the dictates of his conscience.' He was warmly cheered and all agreed that the day would be long remembered by the reformers of Knottingley. [105]

But all was not quite over. His constituency supporters clearly retained fond memories of their former member. Four years later in 1841, Gully found himself being pressed to stand again for election as a Liberal candidate in the forthcoming general election. This time surprisingly he bowed to the pressure and agreed to do so. He decided to stand again at Pontefract in 1841, and declared himself to be the enemy of all monopolies, and the friend of the poor. It was not a wise decision. There was a big swing to Sir Robert Peel's Conservatives.

The citizens of Pontefract, and the neighbouring towns, were far less keen to elect a reforming candidate, and to his chagrin, Gully was beaten in the election by Viscount Pollington. Despite his defeat, Gully still seems to have remained popular in the constituency as there was a further attempt in 1851 to persuade him to stand as the Liberal candidate for election in that year. But by then the allure of political life had lost all its appeal for him and he firmly declined the offer.

---

105 Leeds Times. 22 April 1837

11

The Danebury Confederacy

'The public was completely mystified by the adroit arts of these professors.'

G ULLY did not allow his parliamentary venture to interrupt his career on the Turf. His initial response to the dramatic court case with his former partner Bob Ridsdale, was to announce in 1833 that in future he would associate only with gentlemen, though it is not quite clear what he meant by that. He was confident that the court judgement had done no real harm to his reputation on the Turf and his growing status within the social hierarchy, especially as he was now an MP.

In practice, losing a partner like Ridsdale with his particular skills, plus his unrivalled knowledge of the racing underworld, was a setback for him. It did not take him long to start looking around for a suitable replacement among his acquaintances. He soon reached the conclusion that there were few men better qualified to work with him than one from his blackleg days – the knavish Harry Hill.

Harry Hill

Hill was indeed as big a rogue as Ridsdale and a more uncouth and vulgar one to boot. It was said that if he laid odds against a horse that it would not win, you could be assured that the animal was already doped and probably dead! But he was another leg who had a lot of shrewd common sense where horse racing was concerned and his reputation had not stopped him being hired to carry out a large number of successful commissions for eminent people like Lord George Bentinck (later in 1844 he probably provided Lord George with much of the key information which led to the exposure of Running Rein in the Derby of that year [see Chapter 13]).

Gully and Hill agreed to form an alliance that would operate under the rather sinister name of the Danebury Confederacy. Both were experienced and successful bookmakers, well connected and knew more than anyone about the darker side of the racing world. Together with others who joined them, they were a formidable team and worked together very well without the tensions of the Ridsdale partnership. Under their charge the Confederacy became the most feared and successful horse racing and betting syndicate of the time.

Danebury

The Confederacy based itself on the racing stables at Danebury in Hampshire, which was probably the most important training establishment of the mid-19th century. The stables were run by the Day family – that somewhat notorious dynasty of racing trainers and jockeys we have met before. The Danebury racing stables, paddocks, etc., were reckoned to be perfect for training horses. Lord George Bentinck had established a huge stud there and had invested a great deal of money on the facilities.

The stables sheltered under beech trees at the foot of Danebury Ring and formed a sort of square. Honest John Day remarked that from his residence in the middle, he could take his rounds by means of a door from his sitting room without 'damping his feet'.

The nearby Downs were admirably suited for training racehorses for the white chalk and springing turf were never too hard in the driest of summers, nor too heavy after rain. Consequently the going was nearly always good. The course itself was a round one, a little hilly, but with a straight run-in of three-quarters of a mile which made for a great one to try out two-year-olds. Some 100 people were employed to keep the horses and course in fine condition under the watchful eyes of the Day family. Danebury was without doubt the place where every aspiring racehorse owner wanted to send their horses to be trained.

Gully was well aware that the facilities at Danebury might well give him an edge over other owners and decided that if the opportunity arose, he would definitely want to have his horses trained there despite the doubts about the Day family. Several of Gully's horses in the early 1830s were at the time training at Newmarket and before taking any decisions about moving them to Danebury, Gully decided to spend more time at the town with his friends the Chifney brothers. The brothers were successful trainers with big ambitions and Gully knew that they had set their hearts on winning the Derby in 1834 with their horse Shillelagh.

That particular Derby was hugely anticipated and attracted an unusually large and fashionable crowd. The favourite at odds of 9/4 was called Plenipotentiary, a very good horse, said to be of extraordinary beauty, and it involved Gully in a rather odd incident. Just as Plenipotentiary was being saddled up, Gully stepped forward and offered to buy the horse for a large sum of money, but the owner refused.

Just what Gully's motives were are difficult to pin down. He would have certainly appreciated the potential of owning such a good horse, or it may have been a last-ditch effort to remove it from the race, but if so, it was unsuccessful. After five false starts the race got under way, and in the final stretch Plenipotentiary went clear to win very easily by two lengths from Shillelagh.

In the following year Gully was fortunate to get the opportunity he wanted to move his horses to Danebury. It arose out of the suspicions of Lord George Bentinck the great racing reformer, whose career we will follow in the next chapter. Bentinck had suspected that his large number of horses at Danebury were being trained there by the Days more for their own financial benefit than his.

According to one story, the break came after Bentinck discovered that the trainer John Day Jnr had been deliberately misleading him about the form of one of his horses. While strongly encouraging Bentinck to bet on the horse as a certain winner, Day was secretly advising his own commission agent to wager against the horse as 'he is *hors de combat*, and won't run'. [106] It was just the sort of abuse that Bentinck would later come to devote the greater part of his time and energy to wipe out, and he decided without ado to move all his horses to new stables at Goodwood.

Day, well aware of Gully's reputation as an ambitious owner lost no time to urge Gully to fill the vacant stables with his horses. Gully kept a wary eye on what was going on at Danebury but overall the move proved most successful for him, and indeed for the Day family whose prospects were in danger after the loss of Bentinck's horses.

The Confederacy
The leading lights of the Danebury Confederacy were undoubtedly Gully and Hill, and both owned several horses

---

106 Foulkes, N. *Gentlemen and Blackguards*. p.33

of their own or in partnership with each other, such as Pitsford, Cymba, Hermit, Trumpeter, and other useful horses. However, to broaden their resources they were soon joined by bookmakers Thomas Pedley and Joshua Arnold and a London bill discounter called Mr Turner.

Pedley was a north countryman from Huddersfield, a reputable professional bookmaker who had done well enough to have what was termed a large book. A hearty and popular man, he was well known around the courses for his stentorian voice calling out the odds. He got on well with Gully and later married Gully's daughter Mary Constance in 1850. Pedley also owned several horses and won the Derby with Cossack in 1847 but otherwise had relatively little success on the Turf as an owner.

Joshua Arnold was a bookmaker and betting commissioner who had previously worked closely with both Gully and Hill. He also had horses in training at Danebury. His best horse was one called Sauce Box which unfortunately had left his ownership shortly before it won the St Leger in 1855. Arnold later in his life became deranged and died in an asylum.

As for Turner, little is known about him. He was described as a bill-discounter of an eminent West End type (probably enabling the Confederacy to offer credit to clients at a discount), and he kept a few horses which achieved little.

Overall the Danebury Confederacy was able to wield considerable power and influence over the betting scene. They were always very well informed. They knew a great deal about their own horses and about other people's. If they spotted an opportunity for a good betting coup it was carried out ruthlessly.

William Day was far from being a reliable witness but was probably near the truth in declaring, 'With Hill offering to lay and Gully to back and Joshua Arnold willing to do either or both – all being confederates – the public was completely mystified by the adroit arts of these professors and could not possibly know what would be the course which in their own interest it would be best to pursue.' [107]

The Classic Triumphs

It took a few years for the biggest successes to come, but the late 1840s and 50s saw the Confederacy experience a run of spectacular triumphs which astonished the racing world.

In fact as early as 1844 Gully had also been confident of winning the Derby of that year with his stallion The Ugly Buck – a fine courageous horse which had earlier won the 2,000 Guineas at Newmarket. Unfortunately, all his high hopes were dashed in the infamous Running Rein scandal, which we shall be turning to in Chapter 13.

However, Gully took consolation from knowing that he also had two very promising horses running in the Derby one year later – Weatherbit and Old England. Again, not everything went according to plan. A few days before the Derby was due to be run, Gully got wind of a plot to nobble Old England, one of the favourites for the race. He had heard that a certain Mr Hargreaves of Manchester had bet large sums of money against the horse. Gully was well aware of Hargreaves's very shady reputation in the betting world. Despite Hargreaves denying that he had any private information, Gully was convinced that something fishy was going on at the Danebury stables.

It was said that he descended on the stables like an avenging thunderbolt. With the three Days, old John, and his sons John and William arraigned before him, he demanded an explanation of the rumours. William Day was the main suspect. For a while he withstood Gully's furious interrogation but eventually broke down and confessed that some people at the Danebury stable had indeed been hatching a plot to nobble Old England and that he himself had bet against the horse. It

---

107 Day, W. *Reminiscenes of the Turf. Anecdotes and Recollections*. p.69

Bristol bare-knuckle fighters – they were the superstars of the age

The Fleet Prison 1808 – London's notorious debtors' prison

Henry Pearce the Game Chicken – close friend to Gully and one of the most famous and humane champions of England

John Gully, champion prize fighter 1805–08 – as a young man and great favourite of the Fancy

Bob Gregson, champion of Lancashire – a brave fighter and poet laureate to the bare-knuckle fighters

Newmarket subscription rooms and Jockey Club 1825 – the HQ of British horse racing and where Gully began his racing career

The Betting Post at Epsom Races – a very popular spot where the early bookies and their punters congregated

Bare-knuckle fighting could be a brutal and dangerous sport

John Gully and Bob Gregson square up for one of their momentous fights

John Gully, member of parliament 1832 – Gully takes his seat as the Liberal member for the new constituency of Pontefract

Lord George Bentinck- the Great Reformer – he revolutionised horse racing in the early 19th century

William Crockford – the Shark – and a highly skilled gambler and great rival of John Gully

Gully's Derby winners. Top left to right: St Giles 1832, Pyrrhus the First 1846, and Andover 1854

The Durham Coalfield – Hetton Colliery 1822 – one of Durham's most famous collieries and where Gully invested heavily

John Gully – aged 77

is easy to imagine Gully's fury at the news. It was said to be a very long week before Days got over the 'tornado of fierce wrath and sarcasm which flamed from the indignant victim of the frustrated Conspiracy'. [108]

On the day of the Derby the stewards of the Jockey Club met to discuss the case and summoned William Day up before them. He confessed that he knew that immense amounts had been bet against Old England winning and that he had been instructed by a Mr Bloodsworth, a close friend of the family, and a Mr W. Stebbings, to make the horse safe, and even prevent his appearance at Epsom.

Various means of doing so had been proposed and some tried without any success; for example bruising the foot of the animal so as to lame him and if that didn't work, wrapping a silk handkerchief several times round his leg and beating it until a sinew was sprung.

Finally, if everything else failed, the solution would have been to poison the corn fed to the horse so Old England's intestines would become inflamed and render him unfit to race. Stebbings also confessed that he had for several years received information from William Day about the quality and condition of horses in training at Danebury and had bet heavily for himself and Day.

The stewards, after considering all of the evidence, ordered Bloodsworth, Stebbings and Day to be formally warned off, meaning that they were indefinitely banned from any involvement in the sport. Day continued to argue that the affair was without foundation and that there was never any real intention of maiming Old England. His ban was eventually revoked after just two years.

Perhaps it is not surprising that some years later Day took the opportunity to pen some very unfriendly things about Gully, dismissing him as 'by no means popular with those who

---

108 Thormanby. *Famous Racing Men*. p.36

knew him best on the turf; and though not a bad judge of a horse, was often reputed wise for saying nothing'. [109]

In the event the 1845 Derby ended in another disappointment for Gully and the Confederacy. As usual, a huge crowd of people had gathered to watch the race and after a slow start they made up for lost time by betting more heavily than ever seen since Queen Victoria had come to the throne. The number of horses in the race was the largest ever seen for a Derby, and the betting Ring was described as, 'A horrid chaos and lucre-alluring Charybdis…made up of tens of thousands of civilized beings all intent on preying on their neighbours!' [110]

In the race, Gully's horse, Old England, was badly impeded by a falling horse and finished only third to a much inferior horse called the The Merry Monarch. *The Sportsman* magazine described The Merry Monarch as 'a very bad horse' and his Derby win as the biggest fluke in the history of the race. [111]

In 1846 the Confederacy was triumphant at last. Gully pulled off the outstanding feat of winning the Derby with Pyrrhus the First, and the Oaks with Mendicant. The 44-year-old Sam Day, John Day's uncle, was Gully's jockey on both occasions. It was an exploit that had been accomplished only once before in the annals of the Turf when in 1801 Sir Charles Bunbury's Eleanor carried off both prizes.

Pyrrhus had started second favourite for the Derby at odds of 8/1 in a field of 27 runners. Pyrrhus was not among the early front-runners, but had moved up to join the leading group on the turn into the straight. Day spurred his colt on with a strong run to overtake Sir Tatton Sykes, ridden by Bill Scott, and win by just a neck. Later reports claim that Scott was drunk and in no condition to ride so in fact he should have won the race.

---

109 Day, W. *Reminiscences*, p.65

110 *New Sporting Magazine*. July 1845

111 https://en.wikipedia.org/wiki/The_Merry_Monarch

Mendicant, the winner of the Oaks, was a high quality filly but proved not such a profitable winner for Gully since Lord George Bentinck had bet heavily on the horse to win, so the odds were poor. Mendicant was later sold by Gully to Sir Joseph Hawley for 2,500 guineas. Hawley became an outstanding figure of the Victorian racing scene and went on to win four Derbys.

Although John Day had trained both the Derby and Oaks winners, the success of Pyrrhus must have been something of a bitter pill for him to swallow. He had first bought the horse as a yearling at the Doncaster sales for 300 guineas and then sold a half share in the colt to Gully. The horse had never raced as a two-year-old, and Day, who was short of money, then sold his other share to Gully.

For a few years after his success, Gully's run of good fortune seemed to have deserted him. Then in 1854 he triumphed again by winning both the 2,000 Guineas with The Hermit, and another Derby with Andover. These victories marked the climax of his racing career. The Hermit had never run before the 2,000 Guineas and his gallops at Danebury were going so badly that John Gully was advising some of his patrons to bet against him winning, However, once the colt had gone to Newmarket for the race he seemed to relish the firmer ground and much to Gully's surprise won the Classic for him.

As to the Derby, it was in fact the first appearance of Andover as a three-year-old. There were 27 runners in the field, which also included Gully's The Hermit. Andover was a strongly built bay horse said to be in the bloom of condition, and started as the 7/2 second favourite. Ridden again by Alfred Day, he began slowly before taking the lead in the final quarter of a mile to win by a length, with The Hermit taking third place.

Perhaps the only blemish on Gully's success was the fact that Andover was a colt which he owned in partnership with the notorious gambler and moneylender Henry Padwick. Even Gully, who clearly had few scruples about his choice of allies if there was money to be won, could hardly have picked a more disreputable partner. A rich moneylender, Padwick borrowed from banks at ten per cent and lent at various extortionate rates between 50 per cent and 200 per cent. He became notorious for ruining young men who had become indebted to him. He was also a great gourmet, vain and a blackmailer.

Nonetheless Gully was delighted that two of his horses had taken the first and third places in such a prestigious race as the Derby. Andover's victory was his third Derby success but would be his last Classic winner. Very few have ever achieved such a distinction and it confirmed his reputation as an exceptionally astute racehorse owner and a superb judge of horses. By sheer determination, iron nerve and a cool brain, he had, as one observer put it, 'sapped every obstacle that stood in the way of his progress'. [112]

Now a landed gentleman, with wealth and a large family, he was the very epitome of Victorian middle-class respectability. He was over 70 years old, and the public seemed genuinely pleased to see the old man with his snow-white hair celebrate his triumph. The old suspicions and animosities had largely faded away, leaving the racing scene a sadder place. His famous racing colours, with their jackets and caps in delicate violet blended with white, were rarely to be seen again.

---

112 Mr Gully. *Baily's Monthly Gazette of Sports and Pastimes*. December 1860 p.112

12

Lord George Bentinck

'Lord Paramount of the Turf.'

J OHN Gully's classic successes rightly saw him acclaimed as the 'King of the Turf'. In contrast, however, the overall reputation of horse racing in the 1840s and 50s in England had sunk to a low level. Corruption and villainy were widespread. Evils, such as doping, the bribing of jockeys and officials, and false starts were habitual. Betting had become immense, yet there was no redress against defaulters.

The Jockey Club had been created as the sport's regulatory body but was in the hands of a distinguished oligarchy of aristocrats and rarely spoke with one voice. On big issues, such as the racing of two-year-olds, the control of jockeys or betting, its membership was divided. [113]

The Club, accused its critics, had allowed the sport to be taken over by a horde of determined predators. [114] Horse racing was crying out for reform and the racing public were demanding that the races should be made more attractive and

---

113 Huggins, M. *Flat Racing and British Society.* p.176
114 Ibid. p.187

better organised. It needed someone with the vision, authority and energy to redeem its reputation. Fortunately, in the 1840s the Turf got the man it needed – an aristocrat with immense energy, determination and a love of horses. His name was Lord George Bentinck. No one was better fitted for the task. 'I don't pretend to know much,' he once said, 'but I can judge of men and horses.' [115]

Lord Bentinck

Lord George Bentinck, born in 1802, was the son of the Duke of Portland and a nobleman of very high spirits. He was to have a short and influential political career, becoming leader of the Protectionist cause in the House of Commons. By vehemently opposing the repeal of the Corn Laws, he was mainly responsible for bringing about the fall of the Prime Minister, Sir Robert Peel. However, Bentinck's primary interest in life was horse racing and from the 1830s onwards he embarked on making a series of major reforms that changed the face of the sport.

Bentinck did not make friends easily and as a young man was bored with the incessant round and inconsequential life of London society. One of his pet hates was the social grace of dancing: 'The thought of spending a few hours in an Assembly Hall politely waltzing and cavorting with his female constituents sent him into the depths of misery.' [116]

He craved something more exciting and stimulating in his life, and turned to the Turf. At Danebury in Hampshire, he established what would become the biggest racing stables in England. Beginning with a small and well-selected stud, he gradually increased the number of his 'string', and by the mid-1840s had no less than 40 horses running in public races, and about 100 altogether. Although never fortunate enough

---

115 William George Bentinck. A Web of English History. Web Site.
116 Seth-Smith, M. *Lord Paramount of the Turf.* p.149

to realise his dream of winning the Derby, he was a very heavy gambler and made a considerable amount of money from his betting on the Turf.

Yet he was not necessarily driven by financial greed and wanted above all else to prove his role as the best breeder and owner of horses of the age. He counted, said Greville, the thousands he had won after a great race as a victorious general counts his cannon and his prisoners. [117] He despised others – both wealthy and poor – who were attracted to the sport simply for the purpose of gambling, and none more so than those who had been involved in bribery, fraud, tampering with horses, and even violence. Bentinck was convinced that a concerted attack had to be made on the villainy and fraud that had come to riddle the sport. And just as important, he wanted horse racing to become much more attractive to the general public.

During his racing career, Gully had acted on occasions as a betting commissioner for Bentinck. They knew each other well. There was a mutual respect between the two of them but their relationship was rather wary. Bentinck probably suspected that Gully and his associates, like Hill and Ridsdale, were behind some of the sharp practices he was out to reform but he was never able to pin them down.

The two men were drawn from totally different backgrounds, but had characteristics in common. They were big men in stature, handsome and distinguished-looking. By nature they could be somewhat aloof and reserved. They were invariably polite and courteous but seemed to have few intimate friends. Both were ambitious, obstinate and even ruthless in their determination not to be outdone and very assertive when they believed that right was on his side. They might wager excessively but had sharp calculating minds, though Bentinck could be more impetuous than Gully.

117 Thormanby. *Famous Racing Men*. p.68

And as we have seen, just as Gully was often criticised for his underhand practices, it has to be admitted that Bentinck was not always so upright and straightforward in his own dealings on the Turf.

The Reforms

From the 1830s onwards Bentinck began to use his considerable influence as a wealthy racehorse owner and as a senior Jockey Club steward to drive through changes. With the coming of the railways the public were attending races in much larger numbers and they were demanding big improvements on how they were run and organised. They were frustrated by the lack of information provided for them and the unnecessary disruption. Races rarely kept to time and the starting of races had become notoriously haphazard. And as Gully had found to his cost, open to intimidation and deliberate mayhem.

Bentinck introduced regulations which forced stewards, trainers and jockeys to come out at the agreed starting time of a race and by fining the clerk of the course ten shillings for every minute a start was delayed. False starts were a particular problem that had to be dealt with. The 1830 Derby alone had suffered as many as 14 false starts. Bentinck speeded up the process by ensuring that a man with a flag was posted directly in view of all the jockeys on whom they had to fix their undivided attention and respond to the off without fail, or they would be fined.

Other reforms he brought in included the details of the horses and jockeys to be exhibited on a notice board within sight of spectators, and the custom of saddling and parading horses before the grandstands. He tightened up the procedure for weighing jockeys before and after races which was rife with mischief. Again for the benefit of all spectators, he insisted that all jockeys should be uniformly dressed in silk or velvet or satin jackets and in breaches and boots. Up until then only a small number of owners had registered racing colours which meant that too often jockeys rode in clothes more suited to farm labourers.

Bentinck recognised that betting was an essential part of racing but campaigned hard to rid it of the abuses and villainous practices perpetrated by the cheats, rogues and defaulters associated with it. His particular target was those who defaulted on their bets which by the 1840s had reached epidemic proportions. He did his best to crack down on them, mainly through a policy of naming and shaming. He insisted on the rigid exclusion of every defaulter known to have unpaid gambling debts from the enclosure and grandstand at Goodwood, a practice enthusiastically adopted at other racecourses. On one occasion a man who owed him a bet of £4,000 tried to tempt him to pass over his debt by offering him half of the money. Lord George indignantly refused the proposal, and declared the man to be excluded from all courses until he should pay all his debts in full.

Inevitably Lord George made enemies in the process and he became a target for his more unscrupulous opponents in the racing world. A group of them, mainly out of spite, decided to exploit the chaotically obsolete laws concerning betting which technically limited the amount of gambling winnings and losses that could be made to a derisory total figure of just £10. That was the so-called qui tam statute passed in Queen Anne's reign. Sums of money over that amount were conceivably recoverable and the writs which started to be taken out by Bentinck's opponents under that statute were said to have amounted to nearly £500,000, a sum worth nearly £60m today.

Bentinck's six writs alone stood to lose him £62,500 but other prominent gamblers, including Gully, would also have incurred a very heavy loss if the actions had been declared successful. The sporting interest in Parliament was quickly mobilised and eventually in the 1840s the Duke of Richmond's Manly Sports Bill, which in fact Bentinck had largely drafted, effectively stopped qui tam actions from being taken.

Shortcomings

There were, however, some definite flaws in Bentinck's character. He could be overbearing to the point of arrogance and cruel and vengeful. He fought two duels in his life. One of them was against Gully's friend, Squire George Osbaldeston, over a disputed bet in which Bentinck was palpably in the wrong. Neither was hurt and they were later reconciled.

Bentinck was also accused of being hypocritical. A heavy gambler, he never felt constrained by the strict code of honour he sought to impose upon others. His one-time racing partner Charles Greville claimed, 'The same man who crusaded against the tricks and villainies of others did nor scruple to do things quite as bad as the worst of the misdeeds which he so vigorously and unrelentingly attacked.' [118]

Some of his practices were distinctly sharp. If he thought that he had a good horse at his Goodwood stables, well handicapped and priced to merit a big bet, he would go to extremes to hide its health and training form. In a sport swarming with swindlers and rogues of all kinds, even an honourable man such as Lord Bentinck was prepared at times just like Gully to answer fire with fire.

One improvement for which he was famous worked rather deviously to his own advantage. He invented what was known as the vanning of horses. In 1836 Lord George had won the St Leger with Ellis and it was probably the first time a horse was conveyed in a specially constructed van from the training stable to a racecourse. Before then horses had to go by road and this could take a long time and involve many risks of lameness, chills and expenditure.

118 Huggins, M. *Flat Racing and English Society*. p.108

For example, the distance from Goodwood in Sussex where Ellis was trained to the course at Doncaster, was 250 miles, a distance that would normally take up to three weeks. No one had expected Ellis actually to take part in the St Leger though he continued to be supported in the betting, which led to considerable confusion until Bentinck's plan came to be revealed. His mountainous carriage or caravan was able to be drawn at high speed by a team of six horses whose members could be replaced at regular intervals.

Ellis, and a travelling companion called 'The Drummer', were loaded into the padded interior of the caravan and transported to Doncaster in less than three days! There was even time to pause and give the horses an exercise gallop at Lichfield racecourse on the way.

The project had been kept a close secret and Bentinck and his supporters would no doubt have taken advantage of the generous ante-post price available on the horse. In fact, Ellis, fresh for the race, started at odds of 7/2 in what was an unusually strong field. Ellis took the lead at halfway and won easily without being challenged seriously. Lord George and his connections were reported to have taken approximately £24,000 in winning bets on the race.

Bentinck's obsession with horse racing came to an abrupt end. At the Goodwood meeting of July 1846 he shocked the racing community by announcing that he was retiring from horse racing and selling his bloodstock of three stallions, 70 brood mares and nearly 100 yearlings and foals for the insignificant total of £10,000 – a price well below their market value.

Just why Bentinck took such a sudden step has been the subject of much debate. The majority view is that as the leader of the Protectionist party in Parliament, he decided to concentrate on his political affairs. On the other hand, maybe he thought that he had completed his work as a Turf reformer.

And there were others like William Day who put it down to the fact that a recent lack of success in racing simply drove him from the Turf.

Later, the racing world, in gratitude for all Bentinck's efforts to reform the Turf, raised a large sum of money for him by subscription. He passed it on to the Jockey Club to be used for the distressed dependants of jockeys and grooms.

He died aged 46 while walking alone in the grounds of Welbeck in September 1848, seven months after resigning the Tory party leadership. His death caused a sensation and was attributed at the inquest to emphysema and a heart attack brought on by overwork.

Undoubtedly, for all his blemishes Lord George Bentinck was a very remarkable man. Disraeli called him the Lord Paramount of the British Turf, and his crusade to reform the Turf proved highly effective and very popular. There can be no better illustration of Bentinck's determination to root out dishonesty, and to bring villains to justice, than the role he played in the scandalous Derby of 1844.

13

Running Rein

*'A most atrocious fraud has been
proved to have been practised.'*

THE 1844 Derby was probably the most crooked Classic
race ever run. It dramatically encompassed several of the
crimes, deceptions, substitutions and swindles which
had come to infect the racing scene. It was a scandal which saw
both Gully and his arch rival Crockford, for all their guile and
worldly knowledge, both caught out by the villainy involved,
and in the process they suffered heavy financial losses.

The Derby was, and remains, the leading English race for
three-year-old horses. Only the best of young horses can cope
with the mile and a half of the undulating and demanding
Epsom course. Apart from the prestige that went with the
winning of the race, the Derby had become by the early 19th
century a major betting focus for the whole country involving
stakes of very large sums of money, and as such, a prime target
for unscrupulous gangs.

The race always attracted numerous horses, often quoted
well before the race with very long odds. The nobbling of

horses or their substitution by ones which were older, stronger and more mature was a constant threat. When Queen Victoria made her one and only visit to Epsom to see the 1840 Derby, it was strongly rumoured that the winning horse, Little Wonder, was four rather than three years old, but no official enquiry was made or any objection lodged.

Substitutions

However, the 1844 Derby was very much worse. Not only was there doping and perjury, but two attempts were made to illegally substitute three-year-old colts with older horses. The substitutions had already been rumoured for some time before the race in the racing press, and strong formal objections led by Bentinck and other owners were made in the week before the Derby. Despite the fact that both the owners of the suspect horses were notorious for fraud, both the Epsom stewards and the Jockey Club strangely refused to take any decisive action, much to Bentinck's disappointment.

The horse at the centre of the controversy had been entered under the name of Running Rein and to experts like Bentinck was firmly believed to be a substitute. Until a few months before the race the horse had been owned by a notorious gambler and confidence trickster named Abraham Levi Goodman. He was later proved to be the main man behind the planning of what was an audacious fraud. The other horse suspected to be a substitute was called Leander, owned by the German horse dealers, the Litchwald brothers, a shady pair of men who had earlier been accused in Germany of running horses under false pedigrees.

Goodman and his associates had plotted to steal the 1844 Derby as early as 1841 when they purchased a yearling colt later known as Maccabeus. It came from a good pedigree as his sire Gladiator had finished second in the Derby. Their plan was to enter the horse for the 1844 Derby under another name and as the horse was actually a four-year-old and stronger, it stood a very good chance of winning the race.

By betting heavily especially at the ante-post stage, they stood to make a vast amount of money. To complete the fraud they needed to get a younger, genuine horse with a pedigree and appearance that would support the illegitimate claim of the older horse, so they purchased a thoroughbred named Running Rein and it was under that name that Maccabeus would run.

The Contenders

The two actual favourites for the race were the The Ugly Buck and Ratan. The Ugly Buck was half-owned by Gully and John Day Snr, and trained at Danebury. Earlier in 1844, The Ugly Buck had won the 2,000 Guineas impressively at Newmarket and was described by Lord Chesterfield as the finest horse he ever saw.

The other favourite Ratan, was owned by William Crockford who considered him to be the best horse he had ever owned. Crockford was in his 70s, his health was failing, and he knew it was his last chance of winning the great race. Ratan was attracting a lot of support in the betting, not least by Bentinck who was convinced that Ratan had the beating of Gully's horse. However, Gully and the full might of the Danebury Confederacy began to pour money on The Ugly Buck, causing many of the more astute gamblers to suspect that Ratan was not going to be allowed to win. And Gully, so it was whispered, 'was going to make certain that he did not'. [119]

The railways were booming and an immense crowd of almost a quarter of a million people had gathered to watch the race on Wednesday 22 May and the police had great difficulty in clearing the course before the start. The fact that the Derby

---

119 Blyth, H. *Hell and Hazard.* p.169

was bringing the two great rivals of the Turf – Gully and Crockford – into a final showdown, added to the excitement. The betting odds on the two favourites stayed remarkably even at 3/1 and it was only in the last few minutes before the start that The Ugly Buck became the sole favourite at 5/2. Bentinck also had a horse running in the race called Croton Oil but it was reckoned to have little chance.

However, it was the heavy betting on Running Rein that caught the punters' attention. Less than a week before the race odds of 20/1 or more had been quoted on the horse but on the day they had come down to a starting price of 10/1, with Mr Goodman standing to profit by £50,000 if it won. Rumours swept around the betting circles that something fishy was going on. All the misgivings seem to have been confirmed when the highly fancied Ratan appeared on the course with something badly wrong with his physical condition. The horse could barely make a gallop. As one observer dramatically reported, 'His coat was standing like quills on the fretful porcupine, his eyes dilated, and he shivered like a man with the ague.' [120]

Beyond doubt, Ratan had been got at. Crockford had anticipated that there might be trouble but he was too ill to do anything about it. As for Gully, he may have known more about the situation than he would care to disclose, and remained confident that The Ugly Buck would still win.

The Race

With 29 horses in the race it took three attempts for the starter to get it underway. The pace was blistering from the start but Running Rein soon moved through the field and rounding Tattenham Corner the horse had clearly established its authority. Much to the astonishment of the crowd both the two favourites were being well left behind. In the final straight

---

120 Seth-Smith, M. *Lord Paramount of the Turf*. p.99

Running Rein proved too strong for any other challenger and he won by a length from Colonel Peel's horse Orlando.

The Ugly Buck and Ratan finished a poor fifth and seventh respectively and were said to have been cut up wretchedly. Running Rein and his new owner Alexander Wood, who had bought the horse from Goodman very shortly before the race, had seemingly won the world's most important race, and triumphed over three of the foremost owners of the time – Gully, Crockford and Bentinck.

But it was not to be. When the winning horse and rider reached the winner's enclosure, chaos broke out. They were greeted with raucous catcalls and jeers from the crowd and the bookmakers refused adamantly to pay out to their punters. Urged on by Bentinck, Colonel Peel – brother of the Prime Minister and owner of Orlando, the horse that had come second – then made an official objection and the stewards suspended all bets. Colonel Peel then claimed the winner's stakes on the grounds that Running Rein was not the horse he was supposed to be.

Disqualification

Wood, although the nominal owner of Running Rein, was perhaps not quite as innocent as he claimed about what had gone on, but subsequently sued Colonel Peel for what he still maintained were his legitimate winnings on the race. Bentinck immediately took up the cudgels on Peel's behalf, since he had long been convinced that Running Rein was really Maccabeus. He went about proving his suspicion with great energy, meticulously collecting evidence in support of the case, even to the extent of proving that hair dye had been used to disguise tell-tale marks on the winner's legs.

The court proceedings that followed were held under the famous racing judge, Mr Baron Alderson, and not a man to be trifled with. Wood blandly denied all the charges of deception. Alderson became so exasperated with all the evasive arguments that he demanded of Wood, 'Produce your horse!' After further tedious prevarication, the shame-faced lawyers for Wood admitted that Running Rein had vanished and their client now was prepared to concede that some fraud had indeed taken place. Baron Alderson thereupon instructed the jury to return a verdict in favour of the defendant, Colonel Peel, with the comment, 'Since the opening of the case a most atrocious fraud has been proven to have been practised...If gentlemen will condescend to race with blackguards, they must expect to be cheated.' [121]

Running Rein was thereupon officially disqualified and Orlando declared the winner. Goodman quickly fled to France to escape both the law and his creditors. He eventually returned to London and died in poverty in the 1860s.

Further Skulduggery

The Running Rein saga was not the only piece of skulduggery carried out in the 1844 Derby since it emerged that both Gully's horse, The Ugly Buck, and Crockford's, Ratan, had indeed been doped. Both men had bet heavily on their horses and lost a great deal of money. As regards the other horse believed to be a substitute, Leander, he broke a leg during the race and was subsequently found to be a four-year-old. His German owners – the Litchwald brothers – later admitted that he was actually six.

William Crockford was devastated by the news of the events. He was a sick and tired old man who had not been well for some time and his wife had forbidden him to make the arduous journey to Epsom. When he heard that his colt Ratan had lost, he knew that his life's ambition to win the Derby had gone forever. His only consolation was the news that even the pride of the Danebury stable seemed also to have been nobbled.

---

121 Annual Register. 1844 Vol.86. p.352

Crockford died three days after the Derby. His last words were, 'I have been done – that was not Ratan's right running.' [122]

Some years later there arose an interesting sequel to the story, which suggests that Mr Hargreaves – the man from Manchester whom Gully had suspected of being behind the abortive attempt to nobble his horse Old England before the 1845 Derby – was in fact also responsible for the downfall of Ratan.

The sports writer 'Sylvanus', while drinking with 'Old Crutch' Robinson in The White Bear in Piccadilly, inquired who was the 'lucky, screaming gentleman, with the large face and pink eyes'. Old Crutch simply replied, 'Hargreaves, that's who. Why, four year ago he had not four shilling. That's who he is.' Sylvanus was surprised, and in answer to a further question on how then did Hargreaves get all his money, Robinson replied, 'How did he get it; why, by going for the gloves, man…and by nobbling Ratan, that's how he done it. He was put in by his pal, Sam.' [123]

Presumably, Robinson was making reference to Sam Day.

122 Blyth, H. *Hell and Hazard.* p.185
123 Sylvanus. *The Bye Lanes and Downs of England.* pp.127/8

14

At Home

'We had no skulking host, best be assured, but the most entertaining one and liberal alive.'

W E KNOW relatively little about Gully's life outside his work. He was always a busy man and during the summer racing season, he would have been away from home for much of the time. But having a secure and supportive family undoubtedly meant a lot to him, a lesson brought home to him during his spell of imprisonment as a very young man. Gully could appear rather stern at times but all the evidence suggests he was a faithful and good husband to both his wives.

The loss of several of his many children at a very early age grieved him deeply and he took great care to ensure that those that did survive had the chances in life denied to himself. When he drafted his will when he was nearly 80, he was careful to ensure that the interests of all his grandchildren were also covered.

Mary Mealing

Looking back on Gully's first marriage to Mary Mealing, when he was a young man, it is difficult to know just how happy and successful it had been. Some commentators poked fun at Mary's rather common ways. Charles Greville, for example, thought she was a coarse, vulgar woman, and as Gully moved up the social ladder she may well have had difficulty in adjusting to new manners and ways. However, the fact is the marriage survived for 20 years the trials and tribulation they had to face as a young couple, and by all accounts they had a good relationship.

A little older than Gully, Mary bore him 12 children in the space of 21 years. Unhappily, though very common at the time, several died in infancy. There is no reason to doubt that she was a good mother. As for the children who did survive, records suggest that Gully made sure they received a good upbringing and education.

One of their daughters, Eve, although only five when her mother died, as she grew up proved to be exceptionally helpful to Gully both domestically and with the entertainment of her father's guests. Eve accompanied her father when he and his new wife later moved to Ackworth. When she was 22 she married a local solicitor called Thomas Belk. The Belk family later inherited a fine picture of Gully, soon after he became the boxing champion of England, painted by Samuel Drummond. The picture is now in possession of the National Portrait Gallery, and displayed at the Bodelwyddan Castle in Denbighshire.

Mary Lacey

It was on a business visit to Yorkshire that Gully first met the lady who was to become his second wife. Her name was Mary Lacey. The Laceys of Easingwold were an old northern Roman Catholic family that could trace back their ancestry hundreds of years, perhaps even to the time of William the Conqueror.

The family had been responsible for building an important monastic house and several churches which were desecrated and pulled down in the 16th and 17th centuries. William de Lacey, a martyr of the 16th century, was said to be a former member of the family. But the fortunes of the family had steadily declined and by the time John met Mary, the Lacey estate had been reduced to what was known as the old Manor House, a building which looked like, and probably was, little more than just another country inn.

The story of how Gully first met Mary has a romantic air about it. He was travelling by coach or post-chaise to the races at York when he made a detour to call on a friend. On resuming his journey, as he passed through the village of Easingwold he caught sight of a very pretty girl wearing a plain, cream dress with a blue sash. Beneath a light straw bonnet, tied on with ribbons, was a face that he found to be most 'arresting and expressive'. [124]

Gully was said to have fallen in love with her at first sight and contrived to stay at the Manor House for a night. In the evening after supper, John was invited to join the family in their own private parlour where he was entertained by Mr Lacey, his wife and their three daughters, of whom Mary was the eldest. He was struck again by her beauty and accomplishments, not least her singing, and was determined to ask for her hand.

Although John was over 20 years older than Mary, as a handsome, well-mannered and rich man, he was a highly suitable suitor, and soon had the approval of Mary's parents for the marriage. He was well into his middle age but still healthy and energetic. Charles Greville found him an imposing-looking man, describing Gully as, 'In person tall and finely formed, full of strength and grace, with delicate hands and

---

124 Quinn, M. *John Gully of Ackworth Park*. p.102

feet, his face coarse and with a bad expression, his head well set on his shoulders and remarkably graceful and dignified in his actions and manners. Totally without education, he had strong sense, direction, reserve and a species of good taste which has prevented his behaviour from ever transgressing the bounds of modesty and respect.' [125]

Mary was very happy to accept John and they were married in the village of Easingwold in Yorkshire in May 1828 shortly after the Derby meeting of that year. Greville was much more civil about Gully's second wife than he had been about the first, observing that Mary 'proved as gentle and womanlike as the other was the reverse and who was very pretty besides'. [126]

Ackworth

Gully and Mary were living at Upper Hare Park near Newmarket where their first son Richard was born in 1829. Shortly afterwards they decided to sell the property. Mary was keen to return to Yorkshire, and Gully's interests outside Newmarket were increasingly taking him away to the north of England. He had horses in training in Yorkshire, and regularly attended the Doncaster and York racecourses.

There were also the business opportunities in the north that he was anxious to follow up, not least those related to the booming coal mining industry. Upper Hare Park was therefore sold to Sir Mark Wood for a handsome profit and Gully was able to buy a fine country house and estate at Ackworth Park, near Pontefract, for £21,000. It was a large sum of money, but affordable, and the house was bigger than Hare Park, with a good range of stables, outbuildings and a farm. Its facilities and location suited John and Mary perfectly.

---

125 Greville, C.C. extract from The Diary Review, April 2014.
   Website
126 Ibid. p.110

Gully's second marriage by all accounts was a happy one with a large, and on the whole, healthy family. It was socially successful. Gully, with his dignified manner, intelligence and commanding presence settled quickly into the role of a typical well-respected English squire. Several other well-to-do gentlemen had residences nearby and Gully was able to enjoy the company of many friends and business acquaintances.

Moreover, Ackworth is very close to Pontefract, and when Gully came to be elected to Parliament in 1832 for the new constituency his status in the local community was much enhanced. Then to cap it all, just a few years later he had the honour of being presented at court by Lord Morpeth at a royal levee, and was said to be present in the Queen's drawing room on the following day. Whether the Queen was keen to have him there is open to speculation. No doubt there would have been many present who were piqued to see a common prize fighter and a bookmaker given such social distinction. But it was at least a sign of some levelling in the nature of English society.

Gully had not always been popular with the monarchy. A story did the rounds that he galloped past George IV in the Royal Stand at Ascot without taking his hat off and had compounded his error by making some critical remarks about the arrangements at the royal course. Consequently, Gully found himself barred from running a horse in the Gold Cup for a time, an unreasonable punishment for which the King was later heavily criticised.

His new wife Mary was also very pleased to be back nearer to her family and to renew her acquaintances in the locality. She soon established her own circle of friends, all of whom, so it was said, met with Gully's approval. They entertained regularly, and Gully was regarded as a generous and genial host. He liked to serve the finest food and wine and was especially fond of carving his own joints of meat, as perhaps befitted a man who at one time had been in the butchery business.

Sylvanus, a prominent sporting gentleman of the time who sometimes dined with Gully, has left us with this account of his hospitality, as well as some remarks about his character, 'A good cook, claret from Griffith, with an entertaining and gentleman-like host, he left little to be desired at the dinner awaiting us. Mr Gully is justly esteemed, having raised himself from the lowest paths of life to the position, not merely of wealth, but to that of intimacy amongst gentlemen...I was most gratified by his manly openness, and lack of all sensitive false shame, on any occasional appeal being made to the bygone.

'He, on the contrary, entered freely into many entertaining portions of his history, answered all my questions con amore, and with perfect good nature, as to his mode of training, hitting so as not to injure the hand, wrestling, and other minutiae of the ring...The turbot came from Billingsgate by express, and haunch from his own park. Moet purveyed the champagne, Marjoribanks the port, and Griffiths the cheese. We had no skulking host, best be assured, but the most entertaining one and liberal alive.' [127]

Nor was the family short of servants to look after them at the hall. The 1851 Census records show that also resident at the property were a butler, groom, footman, lady's maid, cook, kitchen maid, and two housemaids.

Children

Gully's marriage to Mary Lacey turned out to be as prolific as his first one. They had 12 children, and all except two survived into adult life. Gully was a proud father, and did what he could to give all his sons and daughters a good start in life. The boys seem to have been well-educated – the 1851 Census shows that

---

127 Sylvanus. *Bye Ways and Downs of England*. pp. 90/92

three of them, John, William and Henry, were all scholars at St John's school in Wakefield.

Several of his sons went on to take commissions in the army or navy as young officers. Richard, the eldest son, and William Gully both saw service in the Indian Army. William rose to become a lieutenant colonel with the Bengal Artillery, and was awarded a medal after the Indian Mutiny. Both Philip and Samuel served as officers in infantry regiments. And Henry joined the Royal Navy and reached the rank of a commander before working with his father on his coal mining interests.

An exception was their son John who practised as a barrister. This led to some sources claiming that the Speaker to the House of Commons who was appointed in 1895 – a Mr William Gully – was related in some way to Gully's barrister son. That was incorrect, and it probably arose from the fact that John was a member of the same legal circuit (the northern) as the new Speaker of the House.

There were six daughters from his second marriage, of whom four survived childhood and were sent to board at the Bar Convent School in York. The school, first founded in 1686 as a boarding school for Catholic girls, had a high reputation and Gully's daughters would have received a sound education there. They later made good marriages into the gentry. Their daughter Eliza unfortunately died at the same school when she was only 13.

Gully was particularly fond of his daughter Mary Constance, known as Polly, who was the eldest daughter of his second marriage. She later married Thomas Pedley, a close friend of Gully and one of his partners in the Danebury Confederacy. Very few letters of Gully remain though he is said to have written several about his time in the House of Commons. Bernard Darwin, a biographer of Gully, was given access to two of Gully's letters to Polly written when her father was an elderly man, and these are reproduced below. [128]

Written in a lively and affectionate manner, and a little waspish at times, they reflect the determined character of the man as well as some of his opinions:

Ackworth Park
Wakefield
Nov 8 1850

My Dear Polly,

I thank you for your kind letter reminding me of my promise, but from what your dear husband told me I fully expected to find you here, and was much disappointed, otherwise I might have given you a call. I wish I could but get quick of this cough, it is not so bad as it was but much worse than it was at Newmarket. Patience and a little of Auld Mary's assistance may soften it. You and Annie must try your best in that way for me.

I shall try old Lomax to say mass for me. What will he charge. The papers are very amusing just now. We should be very dull without them. It is quite nuts (?) for me to see the Pot & Kettle piping at each other, Bye the bye, my darling child, is your beautiful Turkish carpet arrive safe. I suppose so and put down very neatly. I fancy it would just fit my dining room.

Well but about my visit to Stubbing [Stubbing Court, near Chesterfield where the Pedleys lived] at present I cannot fix on any time as I have to be at York on the 13th inst. As soon as I can I will.

I have no doubt Pedley is returned ere this. Please present my best regards and love to you all. I have sent

128 Darwin, B. *John Gully and his Times*. pp.206/210

over to Pontefract to know if Charlie is gone if not to return to him, he is of no use whatever to you and will suit Willy when he gets home. Indeed he will be disappointed if he is gone and as he is doing so well this half at school I should not like to disappoint him. The Honbe. B.R. Lawley is the liberal candidate for Pontefract, as they call him. I have little faith in sons of the Upper House but Moorhouse of course is most enthusiastic – also most if not all of my Pontefract friends. It is strange to me to think what effect the taint of a Lord has on the minds of some folks.

I got a letter from the candidate this morning in bed requesting me to come over by 9 o'clock this morning to join him in the canvass. No I thank you. Stating how well he is getting on in his canvass, if so what he can want of me. I wrote him a letter to say I must decline taking any active part whatever in the Election however inclined I may be. I do not feel well enough. Your Hubby will be written to I expect to become a candidate as they must have another if possible.

I am

Your ever affectionate Father

Jno. Gully

Marwell Hall
Winchester
Sept 9th 1857

My Dear Polly,

I have just received your letter and beg to say that you need not feel annoyed at what have been told me respecting the conduct of your Brother during his stay with you as that has not made no difference in my conduct towards him. I should not even have mentioned it to your mother only that I had requested her to write to you before I went to the north requesting you to invite him to come and stay with you for 10 days or a fortnight. I asked her if she had written and said no. I then said I was glad of it. She asked why and I told her; she wished to know who told me, I refused to give her that information and that I refuse to you but I told he as I tell you that it was not Pedley – oh she said it was the B – s I then declared to her as I do to you that it was not.

After this I hope Pedley will not feel annoyed or you either I have plenty to annoy me at present without anything of that kind.

I thank you and dear Pedley for your kind invitation which I should have been most glad to have accepted but I am not going to Doncaster. We have letter from Poor Willie that troubles me greatly.

That spaniel I do not want, I have two made me a present of by Mr Long. Many thanks to him for his kind offer and also for all your kindness in thinking of me on my birthday. With best love to you all

I am

my very dear daughter

Your ever affectionate Father

Jno. GULLY

The death of another of his daughters, Emily, very soon after her birth in 1844, illustrates just how resolute a man Gully could be once he had made up his mind. The parson of the local Anglican church, St Cuthbert's, at Ackworth, refused to allow a Catholic funeral service for the child to be held at the church graveyard and for her to be buried there. This deeply upset his wife, Mary, who was a devout Catholic. When the news reached Gully he was furious and within an hour had made arrangements to buy a small piece of land from a local farmer abutting the graveyard. He then had it consecrated by a priest so that his daughter could be laid there to rest. In time this piece of land was to become the private burial ground for the Gully family. Gully himself was buried there together with his wife and some of his children.

It was about the same time as Emily's death that John Gully had to endure another heavy blow. He received confirmation of the news that his son Robert, one the sons of his first marriage, had been brutally murdered in China. He was deeply affected by the news and it was a hard time for all the family. We shall be looking at the circumstances surrounding that tragedy in the next chapter.

Church, Charity and Recreation

Gully does not seem to have been a particularly religious man but as he grew older he showed a growing interest in the opinions of various religious denominations. We hear of him taking the chair at Bible Society meetings, hearing Mass given by the Catholic priest, as well attending discussions at Quaker meetings. [129] It is probable that later in life he decided to become a Unitarian (a rumour that Gully had in fact become a Unitarian minister and kept a chapel on his estate seems unlikely).

While residing at Ackworth Park he took his responsibilities as a landed gentleman seriously. He became a member of the Geological and Polytechnic Society of the West Riding of Yorkshire. He showed his support for local affairs, such as exhibiting regularly at the Pontefract Horticultural Society and winning prizes for his gooseberries, cabbages and artichokes.

---

129 John Gully, MP, boxer, horse racer, bodyguard – Google Groups. Website.

He became well known in the surrounding areas for the kindness he showed to the poor and distressed. In the winter of 1842, the *Leeds Times* noted that he had been distributing a quantity of beef among the poor families of Ackworth. In 1834 Gully helped establish the Pontefract branch or lodge of the Loyal Ancient Shepherds – a very popular national movement in the early 19th century which made major contributions to local charities.

It was known, too, that he subscribed to other friendly societies, some 20 in number, in the Pontefract and Ackworth district. John Gully, Esq. it was said, 'was a gentleman in every sense of the word, and many a family in Pontefract had been partakers of the acts of charity and assistance which the worthy gentleman had so plenteously bestowed'. [130]

Predictably, Gully's favourite sporting recreation was horse riding. During his life he had spent many hours travelling around on horseback and he was a very good rider. Few were a better judge of the capabilities of horses, and like most sporting gentlemen of the day it was fox hunting he enjoyed most of all. It became a regular part of his life during the winter months when there was no flat racing. He had first taken up the sport seriously when he was living at Newmarket in the 1820s, and hunted regularly with his friend, Squire Osbaldeston, the master of the famous Quorn Hunt in Leicestershire. By 1834 Gully's performances on the hunting field around the country entitled him to be ranked among the crack riders of England. [131]

When he took up residence at Ackworth Park, Gully transferred his allegiance to the nearby Badsworth Hunt and rode regularly with it. He was a very popular huntsman. A junior member of the hunt called William Whiteley was a vigorous outdoor lad who loved horses and country pursuits.

---

130 *York Herald.* 31 October 1840

131 *New Sporting Magazine.* Vol.8. November 1834

He adored the company of his hero – John Gully – who became something of a role model for the boy.

After a long run, the hunt always called at the nearest gentleman's house for refreshments, and enjoyed the customary crust of bread, piece of cheese and ham, and the home-brewed ale. Gully must have seen something of promise in William and made a point of seeing that the boy was not overlooked at such occasions. They became friendly.

Once when William was working in a field, Gully rode up and asked him if he thought he could catch one of the ponies running loose in the next field. Gully said that if he could catch the pony, then he could ride him home and keep him. It was a challenge impossible to miss, and William at once fetched a rope, and after a hard struggle, secured the pony and rode him home in triumph. [132]

Gully had once owned a good horse called Jack Ketch, and which later gave rise to a curious story that he would have found amusing. After Gully's stud at Danebury was sold, a Melton Mowbray huntsman whose new horse was much admired, announced that it had once been called Jack Ketch and had been owned by Gully, and, he added, there never was a better horse. Another man then said, 'My good sir, you surely must be crazy, for the horse I am now riding is Gully's Jack Ketch. I bought him from Milton, who purchased all Gully's horses.' Only a few days later a third, and then a fourth, Jack Ketch turned up! [133]

It later transpired that the original horse dealer, knowing that Jack Ketch had a marvellous reputation, liberally used his name each time, so that eventually no one could justifiably claim to own the original horse.

Another sport which briefly caught Gully's attention in his younger years was cricket. He rarely played the game and

132 Stratmann, Linda. *Whiteleg's Folly: Life and Death of a Salesman.*
133 Blew, W. C. *The Quorn Hunt and its Masters.*

didn't understand all its intricacies but there is evidence that he occasionally attended the Lord's cricket ground to see it played. In the early 1800s, cricket could be a pretty unruly game, closely contested and often ending in uproar and confusion. But it was popular with wealthy sporting types, and no more so than Gully's friend Squire Osbaldeston, a man hailed as the best shot, cricketer, horse rider and sportsman in England.

Perhaps Gully saw an opportunity to broaden the scope of his betting interests and he may well have taken occasional wagers on the result of a match or on the individual performances of the players.

Marwell

In 1851 Gully decided to sell Ackworth Hall to his Danebury partner Harry Hill for £21,500, near enough the same price he had originally bought it for some ten years earlier. It must have been a great wrench for the family, and especially his wife, to leave Yorkshire. Perhaps he felt that he had outlived the locality. He was no longer a Member of Parliament and he wanted to be closer to his racing headquarters at Danebury in Hampshire where by now most of his best racehorses were being trained.

He rented a splendid house in Marwell, near Winchester, of considerable historic interest. Marwell Hall was built for the Bishop of Winchester around 1320 quite possibly on the site of an earlier hall. It had been entirely rebuilt in 1816 by the Long family. Tradition asserts that the old house was the scene of a secret marriage between Henry VIII and Lady Jane Seymour in 1536. Gully could have scarcely acquired a grander and more desirable residence.

It was while resident at Marwell that Gully experienced his greatest racing successes. He was, it was said, 'as much esteemed in Hampshire as he was in York'. He was as sharp as ever, and with a mind richly stored with anecdotes, liked to spend many a happy evening at Marwell enjoying the company of his family and his old chums from the racing and boxing worlds. [134]

As for Hill, the purchase of the Ackworth Park estate might have suited him for one reason or another at the time but it was probably more of a speculation on his part and he seems to have spent little time in residence there.

The partnership with Gully had won him a lot of money and the two men remained firm friends. When Gully died in 1863, Hill acted as one of his executors. Nonetheless, Hill seems to have let his fortune waste away on one unsuccessful venture or another. When he died in 1880 he left no will and very little money, much to the surprise of those who knew of the immense wealth he once possessed. Ackworth was apparently the only property left by him to his relatives.

15

Robert Gully

'I wish to God we could get anywhere
out of this place and move every day.'

THE greatest tragedy in John Gully's life was the death
in China of Robert Gully, one of the sons of his first
marriage.

Robert was born in 1816 at Newmarket where John and
his first wife Mary Mealing were resident at the time. Unlike
several of his brothers and sisters, he survived his childhood
years in reasonably good health but we know little about his
early years.

Gully would have ensured that Robert received a good
education and the reports and letters Robert wrote before
his untimely death indicate a remarkably lively and well-
informed intelligence. Like virtually all of John's sons he had
an adventurous nature and was well-regarded.

He left home as a young man to travel and work abroad,
though we know that he kept in touch with his family and that
of Gully's second wife. He was also a witness to his sister Eve's
marriage when she was living at Ackworth in Yorkshire. He

soon found himself in the Far East where he was engaged in various commercial activities.

It is very likely that Robert was associated one way or another with the British East India Company which had extensive trading interests in that region. In particular, by the early 19th century it had monopolised the huge and very profitable opium trade out of Calcutta to China. Consequently, millions of Chinese had become addicted. In some coastal provinces, it was estimated that some 90 per cent of Chinese adults had become opium addicts by the mid-1830s.

The Opium Wars

The Opium Wars arose from the attempts by the Chinese authorities to suppress the trade, which was causing serious social and economic disruption in their country. In March 1839 the Chinese government confiscated and destroyed more than 20,000 chests of opium, some 1,400 tons of the drug, that were warehoused at Canton by British merchants. As a result the British government decided in early 1840 to send an expeditionary force to China to protect its interests and to punish the Chinese.

It was Robert Gully's misfortune to become caught up in what was the first of the Opium Wars, from 1839 to 1842. He was working in China and Robert may well have had some commercial interest in the trading of the drug. Eager for adventure, he decided to join the British expeditionary force when it arrived in the region. It consisted of some 17 men-of-war ships as well as four armed steamers sent by the East India Company. In addition a small armada of nearly 30 troopships arrived bearing three fighting regiments.

The British also commissioned a new steam ship, the *Nemesis*, a secret weapon which was to baffle and shock the Chinese soldiers. The ship, although carrying far fewer cannon than most fighting ships of the Royal Navy, proved decisive in the war. It could move easily against the wind, and it proved admirably suited to navigating the mud flats and sand bars of the river mouths of the Chinese ports.

Robert succeeded in joining the *Nemesis* in 1840 on a temporary basis. He soon acquitted himself very well. There are accounts that he played a distinguished part in the taking of the port of Ningbo and in other battles in which the ship was engaged. His brother officers were very sorry to see him go when he decided to return to the commercial activities which had first brought him to Macao, the Portuguese port on the south coast of China.

Capture

For the voyage back to Macao, Robert took the ill-fated decision to take passage on a private merchant brig called *Ann* which was very likely to have been engaged in the opium trade for some years. It was commanded by a Captain Frank Denham. On the night of 10 March 1842 the brig struck a reef just off the coast of the island of Formosa, now Taiwan, in a severe gale. The crew and passengers were forced to abandon the ship and to take refuge on the shore.

Very soon, armed Chinese forces appeared on the scene with the objective of seizing the shipwreck and the survivors. The survivors were reduced to surrendering, then stripped naked, and put in chains. They had no idea what fate lay ahead for them, but appear to have been reasonably optimistic that they would soon be released. Both Gully and Denham began to compile notes and diaries which recorded in graphic terms details of the country, and the people, they passed on their way. [135]

But their main concern was to record the terrible suffering that they and other captives were having to endure. It was later

---

135 Journals kept by Mr Gully and Cpt. Denham during a Captivity in China in the Year 1842

officially condemned as barbarous and 'so entirely at variance with the principles by which the Chinese profess to be guided in all cases of distress produced by the act of God…and so harrowing from its cold blooded atrocity, that the mind cannot be brought without difficulty to credit, and realise the scenes presented by all its blood-stained record'. [136]

After their capture, all the prisoners were marched south, and passed the ship, the *Ann*, which was in the process of being ruthlessly plundered. Groups of people in soldiers' clothes were coming and going carrying sheets of copper and boxes of dollars, chests of drawers, boxes and clothes. When the prisoners reached a mandarin's premises, they were horrified to be told that they would be beheaded. They were put into small cells, each with 25 men and their jailers. The weather was very cold and there was nothing to lay their heads on but a sprinkling of straw to keep them from the damp bricks. Forced to march on, often in leg irons, they moved from one primitive village to another and continued to suffer all sorts of abuse and hardships.

After several days' march, they reached the capital of the island Ty-wan-foo, where Gully and Denham were separated and put into two different groups. The prisoners were confined to their cells for two months or more and never allowed out to wash or change their clothes. They were, wrote Robert in his diary, 'annoyed by myriads of fleas, bugs, lice, ants and mosquitoes, and centipedes, without a possibility of getting rid of them, except by death or a miracle'. To make matters worse their jailer was, in Robert's words, the most wicked brute that ever was created (Denham seems to have been treated a little better than Gully since the Chinese seemed unable to have any idea of a type of person, like Robert, who did not have some form of official employment).

---

136 Ouchterlony, John. *The Chinese War*. p.497

Gully was soon suffering badly from fever and attacks of piles. He bore the decline in his health with great fortitude. He did not sleep for several nights together. On one occasion he resorted to accepting a piece of opium in an attempt to relieve his suffering. It gave him a brief period of feeling quite happy, but soon made him feel sick and laid him on his back the whole day. From time to time he was interrogated by the mandarins responsible for the capture but Gully found their questions ridiculous and indelicate.

They still persisted with the notion that the *Ann* was in fact an armed vessel rather than a cargo boat. Unfortunately, shortly before the *Ann* had been shipwrecked, another British vessel, the *Nerbudda*, a transport ship, had suffered the same fate, and the local Chinese were convinced that both were part of a planned invasion of the island.

The prisoners were not allowed any exercise, nor books or other amusements to relieve the monotony of prison life. 'I wish to God,' Robert wrote, 'we could get anywhere out of this place and move every day.'

For his own amusement, he began to sketch pictures, for example one of a bear hunt and another of a line of battleships attacking a French fort. Frank Denham, too, took up the same pastime, and both liked drawing European objects, such as railway trains, coaches, ships, tunnels, etc. which were admired by some of the Chinese guards and even bought for a little money. With the cash Gully made attempts to bribe his jailers to help him make contact with the outside world, notably Amoy (now Xiamen) a port captured by the British in 1841.

His letters described the plight of himself and the other prisoners but he received no reply and help never came. Most of the letters were probably never delivered though at least one seems to have been received. Later, some blame was laid at the door of the English authorities in the region for what seemed to be a weak response to the tragedy but the likelihood was that they were simply unaware of the gravity of the situation. It is also possible that senior Chinese officials close to the Emperor would themselves have been deceived by lies from the local mandarins about the conditions in which their prisoners were being held.

Atrocity

The last entry in Robert's diary in August 1842 ends abruptly. It reads, 'Attempted to boil water without fire, but curiously enough failed.' After five months' imprisonment he was still showing what a spirited and courageous man he could be. He seems to have had no anticipation that he was about to be led away to his execution along with the other prisoners.

That terrible event occurred on or about 13 August 1842. Some 197 men from the two ships, the *Ann* and *Nerbudda*, were led out of their prisons and placed on their knees near to one other, their feet in irons and their hands manacled behind their backs. This was in a wide plain just outside the capital of the island where many thousands of Chinese had gathered. All the unfortunate men seem to have been unaware of why they had been brought there. Then a group of executioners appeared and with their heavy swords systematically beheaded the prisoners. Their heads were placed in small baskets and carried away to be exposed on the seashore and their bodies thrown together into one common grave.

If we take into account both the crews and all the other people who were on board the *Nerbudda* and the *Ann* when shipwrecked, the total number of around people barbarously killed by the Chinese authorities was probably 300. Only two survived, one of whom was Captain Denham. The whole brutality had simply no justification. The Chinese continued to brand the prisoners as foreign barbarians, whose invasion of their territory had been thwarted by the valour of Chinese sailors and troops.

The official news of the outrage reached the British government soon after the Treaty of Nanking, which ended the first Opium War, was signed on 29 August 1842. Sir Henry Pottinger, Her Majesty's Plenipotentiary in China, was able to do little more than to remonstrate in strong language to the Chinese Emperor, expressing his 'extreme horror and astonishment' of the massacre of the British subjects after the shipwrecks. [137]

He declared that it would remain a stain and disgrace in the annals of the Chinese empire, and he called upon the Emperor not only to punish those responsible, but also to confiscate their property for the benefit of the families of the poor people. He warned the Emperor that without just atonement and retribution there might be a renewal of hostilities between the two countries which would be deeply deplored by Britain.

The Emperor replied to the dispatch in weasel words, stating that he agreed in full with Sir Henry's demand and that his imperial majesty regarded alike all 'outside or inside subjects, and that in future due consideration should be shown to all of them'. [138] It seems very unlikely in fact that any retribution by the Chinese ever took place.

Memorial

John Gully would probably have been made aware some time in 1842 that his son was in captivity in China and was naturally very anxious to learn news of his fate. Early in the following year, rumours reached him that his son had been murdered and in desperation he requested Lord George Bentinck to use his influence at the Foreign Office to discover if they were true. He and his family were shocked when the official report confirming Robert's death reached them.

---

137 Cunynghame, A. *The Opium Wars*. p.187
138 Ibid p.189

Gully was not one to outwardly show much emotion but he must have grieved deeply. He ensured that a memorial plaque to his lost son was placed prominently on the south wall of St Cuthbert's Church in Ackworth. It reads:

'Sacred to the memory of Robert Gully, son of John Gully, Esq., who, after suffering the horrors and privations of shipwreck on the Island of Formosa, in the brig Ann, on the night of the 10th of March, 1842, in which vessel he was passenger; he was, together with the rest of the crew, taken prisoner by the Chinese, and suffered the greatest privations and hardships, which he bore with the most exemplary fortitude, manly and cheerful resignation, to about the 13th of August, when he, together with about 300 other British subjects, was most barbarously murdered in cold blood by the Chinese authorities, in the town of Tywan Foo, aged 28 years. He was endeared to a large circle of friends for his manly virtues and kindness of heart. This tablet was erected by a bereaved and afflicted father.'

Knowing what we do about Gully's character, it seems very likely he would have pressed his political contacts to take some severer measures against those responsible in China for the atrocity. However, apart from Sir Henry Pottinger's protest there is no record of any other government action taken.

When Captain Denham later returned safely to England, he quickly made contact with John and his family to express his condolences and his deep admiration for Robert. There is an interesting letter that John wrote in February 1844 which suggests that Denham may have even been a relation of Gully, perhaps a husband to one of his sisters-in-law. It is addressed to an official in the House of Commons and reads in full:

'You were kind enough to say you would put my name down on the Speaker's list for tomorrow night's debate. I shall feel further obliged if you will strike out my name and put instead my brother in law, Captain Denham is the Gentleman who commanded the Brig Ann, which was wrecked on the Island of Formosa, and my poor son was a Passenger who was cruelly murdered with 51 of the crew. The above gentleman is going … to China very soon and as he informs me has the case of some things to take out to your son. He never was in the House of Commons to hear a debate will be a great treat to him and I shall feel myself under a great obligation to you.' [139]

In 1867, 25 years after the tragedy, an interview was published in which the British physician William Maxwell asked an old Chinese clerk if he remembered the beheadings. He responded that he did, and claimed that on the same day, a heavy thunderstorm formed and lasted for three days, drowning an estimated 1,000 to 2,000 people. 'I remember that day well,' he said, 'and a black day it was for Formosa…that was a judgement from Heaven for beheading the Foreigners; but it was done in revenge for your soldiers taking Amoy.' [140]

139 John Gully. icollector.com. Website
140 https://en.wikipedia.org/wiki/Nerbudda_incident

16

Coal Mining

*'Having become rich he embarked in
a great coal speculation, which
answered beyond his hopes.'*

THE final chapter of John Gully's life took him to the
Durham coalfields. Soon after Andover's victory in the
1854 Derby, Gully decided that the time had come to
retire from racing and to sell his stud at Danebury. He was
over 70 years old, and probably felt that the Turf had little
more to offer him. He would have been conscious too that
times had changed.

A new era of stricter morality and middle-class respectability had arisen since the coronation of Queen Victoria,
markedly different from the world in which he had made
his fame and fortune. But Gully was not a man to rest on
past achievements. He was in reasonably good health, still
ambitious and with interests now focused firmly on the
business world. It was time, he reasoned, to move north once
again in order to look after the large coal mining investments

he had made in the county of Durham. By 1860 he had found a suitable property near Durham called Cocken Hall. It was another beautiful country house built in the 17th century on the banks of the River Wear near Finchale Abbey. From there the collieries at Trimdon, Hetton and Thornley which he had invested heavily in were easily accessible. Cocken, however, was to be his last family residence.

The Durham Coalfields

He had first started to invest large amounts of his winnings from horse racing into the expanding coal mining industry of the north of England around the time he was elected to Parliament in 1832. It was in County Durham where he decided to concentrate his investments. Coal was a very rich mineral resource in the county.

It had been mined in substantial quantities even in medieval times in the areas of the Tyne and Wear but the first half of the 19th century saw the opening of many new deep collieries in eastern Durham where the coal lay deep beneath the magnesian limestone. The first shafts to mine the coal were sunk in the 1820s, starting with the opening of a colliery at Hetton-le-Hole to the south of Sunderland. We do not know exactly why Gully chose to invest heavily in coal mining. The industry was booming and it would certainly have been a ready topic of conversation in some of the business circles in which he moved. He was a shrewd enough businessman to recognise that there was good money to be made from mining to meet the insatiable demands of the Industrial Revolution. And he would also have been aware of the huge risks involved. There was no guarantee a new mine would prove successful, and it was a costly and dangerous business in which fortunes could easily be lost overnight. As a betting man, Gully was certainly not risk averse but he would have certainly wanted to weigh up the odds carefully.

Fortunately, two men at the time were well placed to provide him with some useful information about the prospects for coal mining in Durham. William Smith, a geologist widely recognised as the Father of English Geology, had spent some time in the 1820s living in Yorkshire at Scarborough and may well have met Gully on his travels in the county. Smith had some valuable practical experience as a coal mining engineer and surveyor in south-west England, but his importance derives from the outstanding work he did as a geologist.

He produced several exceptionally detailed maps of the rocks and strata of many areas of England including the county of Durham. This map confirmed that the prospects for future coal mining in the east of Durham beneath the limestone were indeed very good. Moreover, the development of steam power in the early part of the 19th century had made it possible to exploit those coal seams at a much deeper level. This was just the sort of helpful information that Gully was looking for.

The other person Gully may well have consulted was a wealthy gentleman called Colonel Bradyll, who owned large estates in Lancashire, Cumberland and Durham. Bradyll knew William Smith and commissioned him in 1821–22 to make a survey of the potential for coal mining on all his estates. Smith had confirmed that the colonel's properties in Lancashire and Cumbria were altogether inferior to the estates which he had scrutinised in Durham. Armed with that knowledge, the colonel had set about making some very profitable investments in collieries in east Durham, including the areas around Haswell and Hetton (unfortunately for Bradyll, some of his other investments were unwise and he was forced into bankruptcy in 1844).

The Hetton Colliery

Colonel Bradyll owned the Hetton colliery and it was there that Gully decided to make his first major mining investment.

Hetton, lying just south of Sunderland, was destined to become one of the most famous colliery towns in County Durham. The sinking of shafts there had begun in December 1820 and coal was finally reached in September 1822. It was high quality coal and there was lots of it.

By November of that year coal was being shipped to Sunderland via the Hetton Colliery Railway – the first to be purpose-built for steam locomotives and an important stepping stone in the career of the great engineer George Stephenson. The Hetton colliery became the first major public company in County Durham.

A rumour suggested that Gully had acquired his shares in the Hetton colliery by a bet but that sort of tale was readily bandied about where Gully was concerned. More likely he bought the shares at a fairly low price – a sum of £2,000 was said to have changed hands – since the pit at Hetton and others in the area still faced immense difficulties. The shafts had to be very deep since the coal seams which lay at the base of the limestone were hard to work. In addition there was a severe risk of water held in a bed of sand pouring into the shafts which could only be overcome by the invention of powerful pumps by Newcomen and Watt.

When Gully invested in the colliery he was joining a partnership which was typical of the time when a major mining development was proposed. A lot of money and expertise were required. A group of directors was needed to finance, develop and even on some occasions manage a colliery. For example, a typical board of directors consisted of the landowner who had acquired the right to mine the coal on his land, speculators like Gully with substantial amounts of money to invest, and someone who knew something about the industry and how a mining colliery should be best organised and run.

Gully joined a group of four principal directors who were the major shareholders at Hetton and had already successfully driven the venture forward. First was Captain Archibald Cochrane of Eppleton Hall, who owned the land (he was a younger brother of Admiral Lord Cochrane, afterwards Earl of Dundonald, and one of the most daring commanders of the Napoleonic Wars). Cochrane was always extremely optimistic about the future of the mine, and may well have been the person who finally persuaded Gully to make his investment in the colliery.

The other three directors consisted of former banker Arthur Mowbray of Bishopwearmouth, George Baker, a very wealthy man of Elemore Hall, and Nicholas Wood, an experienced mining engineer who was later appointed to manage the colliery.

Mowbray was the sort of character whom Gully would have come across frequently in his career. An enterprising banker of somewhat dubious dealings, he had been declared bankrupt in 1815 when the Durham and Darlington Banks crashed in the post-Napoleonic depression. Undaunted, he managed to invest in Bradyll's Hetton Coal Company from 1820 onwards and had successfully cleared his debts. The shares he bought in 1820 at £250 each had appreciated to £18,000 when he finally sold them in 1832 to fund his retirement – a striking example of the scale of the fortune that could be made from coal mining.

The experience and skills that Wood brought to the partnership were highly important. Both he and George Stephenson had been born at Wylam, near Newcastle, and had become close friends. In 1821, the proprietors of the newly formed Hetton Coal Company had been faced with the crucial problem of transporting the large quantities of coal across the countryside to staithes (jetties or wharves built specifically for loading coal on to ships) on the Wear for shipment to the markets of the south.

Under Wood's recommendation, the company invited Stephenson to take charge of laying a railway line from Hetton to the staithes approximately eight miles away, and to be worked by locomotives. The laying of the line was supervised by Robert Stephenson, brother to George, and who later became resident engineer at Hetton colliery. The line took three years to build and it was the very first in the world to be operated by steam locomotives, thus making Hetton a very important part of railway history.

For Gully, coal mining would turn out to be just as profitable for him as was horse racing. By the mid-1830s the price of coal mined at Hetton was fetching a higher price on the London market than any other coal mined in the North East, and Gully was enjoying a substantial profit on his shares. As Thormanby fittingly recorded, Gully having become rich had, 'embarked in a great coal speculation, which answered beyond his hopes, and his shares soon yielded immense profits.' [141]

In contrast, Gully's great rival William Crockford had also been persuaded to invest in a mining venture in Flintshire which was a complete loss – the source of another grudge he had against Gully.

The Thornley Colliery

By the end of 1834, when Gully attended a great dinner in Newcastle given to the Earl of Durham, he had become the largest proprietor of the Hetton colliery and was reported to have invested in it a total of around £160,000, a huge sum worth over £17m today. [142]

However, later in the decade Gully decided to sell his shares at Hetton. Perhaps he felt he had done well enough out of the colliery and sensed that there were even more profitable investments elsewhere.

In 1838 he headed up another ambitious speculation involving investment in the Thornley Coal Company

---

141 Thormanby. *Famous Racing Men*. p.77

142 The *Liverpool Courier*. 27 November 1834

which was engaged in the sinking of the Thornley pits in the Easington district of Durham. This time his main partners were Sir William Chaytor, Thomas Wood and John Burrell.

Sir William, who owned the land, was married to Gully's sister-in-law, Anne Lacey. He was a Whig MP for Durham city and then Sunderland in the 1830s, though notoriously inactive, and must have been a scruffy individual since he was locally known as Tatty Willie. Wood, from Coxhoe Hall, was a mining engineer, and Burrell was a Durham lawyer.

It was to become another very active partnership. All the directors were eager to seek out other potentially profitable investments, especially those associated with transporting coal. In the 1840s they took a close interest in investment in the building of railways which were another highly popular and potentially prosperous venture of the age. They all became members of the provisional committee of a proposed new railway – the Lancashire, Weardale and Hartlepool Railway – and the formal application for an Act of Parliament to construct the line was submitted in 1845. [143]

Interestingly, the application was drawn up by Gully's son-in-law Thomas Belk, a solicitor in Hartlepool. The ambitious project was designed to provide a link for the new port of Hartlepool with other railways serving the important manufacturing centres of Yorkshire, Lancashire and Scotland. It would not, the committee hastened to assure prospective investors, interfere with any gentleman's residence or ornamental property. The investment required amounted to £120,000 to be financed by good shares at £20 each but it is not clear how successful this venture was.

The Thornley collieries proved very prosperous though they took several years to complete. They transformed the locality from a sparsely populated farming community around

---

143 *London Gazette*. November 1845

a manor to a densely populated industrial village with the pit as a focal point. The first houses were often poor, single-storied, limestone cottages with little space and light and huddled together as near to the pit as possible.

Conditions for the men, women and children were very hard. Miners' wages were poor and their hours long and early attempts in the 1830s to organise workers into a union were quickly crushed. The relations between owners and miners at the Thornley colliery were probably no better or worse than others at the time, although it is fair to point out that up to 1843 the colliery had managed to work for nine years without a strike.

Whether Gully and his partners did make any determined effort to improve the local environment or the conditions of the workers is not known. Gully had a sentimental side to his nature and during his life he did show sympathy for the common man. He would not have wished to be branded a man completely and ruthlessly unconcerned about the welfare of the miners, which sadly was too often the case in many collieries of the time. But Gully was also a hard-headed businessman, not inclined to let his emotions come before the need to make a profit from his investments.

However, in 1843 a serious strike broke out at Thornley, by now one of the largest collieries in the country, which does not reflect too well on Gully or his partners. The miners had a number of grievances but the main issue arose from the custom in the industry of binding the men to work for a full year at a particular colliery. Breaking that bond carried severe penalties for the miners and could even result in being deported.

The owners of the colliery at the time were listed as John Gully, Thomas Wood, Rowland Webster and John Burrell and they wanted to extend the length of the bond. After everything else had failed, the miners decided to come out on strike. On 24 November 1843, arrest warrants were issued against 68 men at the colliery for absenting themselves from their employment.

The prisoners were tried at the Durham Assizes and each gave similar evidence about the hardships they suffered under the bond. They were found guilty and they all chose to go to jail rather than to work under the existing bond. The magistrates thereupon sentenced all 68 men to six weeks' imprisonment. However, they were fortunate to be represented by a very able lawyer named William Roberts, who had earlier won several legal battles against the bond. Popularly known as the miners' attorney-general, Roberts's philosophy was simple, 'We resist every individual act of oppression, even in cases we were sure of losing.' [144]

Roberts obtained a writ of Habeas Corpus and the Thornley prisoners were removed to the Court of Queen's Bench in London, where on a technicality they were acquitted. They all returned home to County Durham as heroes but the bond remained in place for the time being.

In 1844, all the miners of the Durham coalfield, including Thornley, were involved in a particularly long and bitter strike which saw them and their families evicted from their tied cottages and labour brought in from elsewhere. The strike caused great hardship and the miners were starved into submission. However, the strike was not entirely fruitless, for it gave the death blow to the yearly bond. It was increasingly replaced in favour of a fortnightly contract of service. And in places where the bond was still retained (as it was in many collieries for another generation) its harsh and one-sided conditions were considerably modified.

After Gully's death, the family kept an interest in Thornley until the early 1890s when it was sold at a healthy profit to a limited liability company called the London Steam Colliery and Coal Co.

---

144 https://en.wikipedia.org/wiki/William_Prowting_Roberts

The possibility of sinking further Durham collieries continued to attract the interest of Gully and his partners. By the 1840s and 50s they were actively investing in the development of the Trindon colliery, near Thornley. Gully eventually sold his share of this colliery to his partner Thomas Wood who then became registered as the sole owner. Sadly, on Thursday 16 February 1882, several years after Gully's death, the colliery was the scene of a large disaster when an explosion occurred in which 74 miners were tragically killed.

The Wingate Colliery

In 1862, just a year before his death, John Gully paid the 2nd Lord Howden £30,000 for the outright ownership of the Wingate Estate and Colliery quite close to Trindon. That sum of money would be equivalent in today's money to well over a million pounds – a striking indication that Gully, although approaching old age, was still prepared to make a very substantial investment. The Wingate colliery was yet another deep mine and it had found excellent coal at a depth of around 400 feet. Mining at the colliery had progressed well, and Gully was clearly impressed with its future prospects.

Wingate proved to be Gully's last major speculation. He died just one year later and left in his will £10,000 for the further development of the colliery. It remained in the ownership of Gully's executors and was administered by the Court of Chancery until 1906 when it was sold for a much larger sum of money than Gully had paid. To the end it seems that Gully had not lost any of his ability to recognise a good investment when he saw one.

The Wingate colliery was closed in 1962 but the village still holds some memories of Gully. There is a street named after him and a community centre named Gully House.

17

Conclusion

*'No man more fairly earned
the respect he gained.'*

IN sporting terms, the period between the 1790s to early Victorian England is often seen as something of a golden age. Horse racing, prize fighting, pedestrianism (foot races), cricket and card games all prospered. They became widespread, better organised and appealed to all levels of society. They also involved a fair share of foolhardy extravagance, wild living, intrigue and roguery.

All of them had gambling – often for very high stakes – as a central feature. Fortunes were won and lost at the turn of a card. It was an era too of great social, political and economic change. The retirement of George III saw the birth of a more wild, frivolous and ostentatious age in which some extraordinary and remarkable people flourished.

Many besides John Gully rose from rags to riches by one means or another. They overcame their disadvantages and had impressive stories to tell. But very few can match the sheer scale and drama of Gully's own achievements. His path from poverty and prison, to his success in the ring, on the Turf, and as a businessman and MP, is fairly well known yet a true picture of the man and his character are much more difficult to pin down. Apart from some letters, his betting records and a very lengthy will, he left very few details of a personal kind. Reliable accounts from people who were closest to him are also lacking, and one is forced back to contemporary opinions and observations. And those opinions are strikingly diverse.

On certain aspects of his character we have general agreement. People praised his great physical courage, his intelligence and his openness. For a man from such a poor background and with very little education, there was an inborn dignity about him. As he matured his rather stern, reserved manner and powerful physical appearance could be intimidating. He certainly kept his guard up. He rarely lost his temper but when he felt someone had unfairly crossed him, his wrath could be fearsome.

He was a man of few words and often silent for long spells, while chewing thoughtfully on his cigar. When he had something to say he showed that he could use his tongue just as effectively as his fists, and once relaxed would be very good company. As one of his contemporaries remarked, 'In his conversation every word weighed a pound, and we never remembered getting so much solid guidance from anyone about old times as we did in a short chat with him when a Heath afternoon was over. No one could sketch his old chums more deftly.' [145]

Similarly, although Gully was not a frequent writer, the few examples available indicate he had no difficulty in expressing himself forcefully and in a lively manner on paper.

No one doubted, too, that Gully was a most determined and ambitious man. 'He must be a sharp chap, and get up early, as beats John Gully, I can tell you,' Hen Pearce had sagely

---

145 The Druid. *Saddle and Sirloin*. p.313

commented after their epic battle in 1805. The fact is that Gully hated losing, whether in the Ring, on the Turf or fighting a parliamentary election. His bankruptcy and imprisonment in the Fleet might well have undermined the resolve of a lesser man but it strengthened Gully's will to succeed in life.

In some ways he was a fortunate man. He was very lucky to be released from prison and his debts paid off. His health was good. He became a bookmaker and colliery owner at just the right time when business was booming.

But he also made his own luck. He had no illusions that sometimes risks had to be taken and he was prepared to learn from his mistakes. But he went about his investments whether on horses, property or coal mines in a shrewd and business like way. His clients trusted him. He freely acknowledged the help he had been given at critical stages of his life.

Even after he had fallen out badly with his former partner Robert Ridsdale, Gully was still prepared to offer him money to help him overcome his difficulties. There was never a hint of infidelity in his two marriages and he ensured that his children were well cared and provided for in their lives. When he settled in Ackworth, he took his position as a wealthy country squire seriously and gave what assistance he could to the poor in the locality and to those with personal difficulties.

Why then did Gully come in for so much criticism? It is true some people did find him too cold and calculating for their liking. He had to face a good deal of prejudice about his poor birth and background. Gully wanted to climb the social ladder, and in the rigid Georgian society, climbing did not make for popularity. Charles Greville's low opinion of his success and of his first wife seems more spiteful than meaningful.

Others like William Crockford were deeply envious of his achievements on the Turf and plotted to take him down. And some like William Day were out for revenge having had their own crooked dealings exposed by Gully. That said, he was undoubtedly a controversial figure and accused by many of being as crooked as they come and having won his vast fortune by unfair and unscrupulous means.

Gully's early experiences undoubtedly did much to mould his character. Imprisonment, prize fighting, and bookmaking as a blackleg, were not ones for the faint-hearted. He found himself pitched into a world where the weakest went to the wall and to survive he had to be prepared to fight that world with its own weapons. If that meant at times being cunning, hard and ruthless, then so be it.

It was a world, too, that inevitably brought him into contact with some very dubious and disreputable characters. But if they were going to be of use to him, he was not prepared to step aside. If you were to judge a man simply on the character of many of the men with whom he worked, then John Gully comes out very poorly.

As a bookmaker and gambler, Gully was accused of practices which by the standards of the present day would be judged illegal and corrupt. He and his close confederates, notably Ridsdale and Harry Hill, pulled off a series of very lucrative betting coups, which many were convinced involved some form of corruption, notably bribery or the invidious practice of laying and backing against dead 'uns. It was practices like those which led to racing historians like Roger Longrigg to denounce Gully as one of the most evil men to be involved in horse racing on the 19th-century Turf. [146]

However, Gully lived at a time when lies, insinuations and slanders could be spread around without fear of penalty and his very success was bound to make him a prime target. Accusations for example that Gully was responsible for the nobbling of famous horses such as Ratan or Plenipo are simply not substantiated by the evidence.

---

146 Longrigg, R. *The History of Horse Racing.* p.113

Importantly, it has also to be understood that the sporting morals of Gully's day were far lower than they are today. The hugely popular sports of boxing and horse racing were infected with scandals and skulduggery and it seems harsh and unfair to single out Gully as any worse than many of his contemporaries. Even the great reformer of the Turf, Lord George Bentinck, 'was not averse to stooping low in his efforts to score financially at the expense of others'. [147]

For all his faults, Gully did have standards which he tried not to fall below. He did mix with some disreputable rogues like Ridsdale and Hill, but had good business reasons for doing so and does not appear to have resorted to their worst forms of corruption. He had some fine and genuine personal qualities. He could be a very generous man and his heart was in the right place. His good manners, discretion and straightforward dealings impressed his patrons and they liked him for it.

And his racing career was not without its failures but he took them in his stride and settled his losses promptly. His success in making a great deal of money on the Turf had just as much to do with his knowledge of horses, the wealthy commissions he obtained, and the network of informers and spies which he built up so meticulously, as to his disreputable practices.

When Gully approached his 80th birthday, his health began to fail. He had to endure an attack of jaundice and was suffering from prostate problems. No longer able to travel, he moved into a town house, though not his own, at the North Bailey, in the centre of the city of Durham. He died there on 9 March 1863 at the age of 79.

He was buried five days later at Ackworth, next to his daughter Emily in that piece of land by the church which he had railed off and had consecrated by a Catholic priest. At the express wish of Gully, his interment was carried out by a

---

147 Seth-Smith, M. *Lord Paramount of the Turf*. p.69

Unitarian minister – Goodym Barmby – from the Westgate Chapel in Wakefield. Gully had become increasingly attracted to the Unitarian movement and Barmby, a man devoted to reform and bettering the conditions of the people, was one of the best-known ministers in the West Riding of Yorkshire.

At the time of his death, Gully had become one of the most honoured and respected gentlemen in the north of England. On the day of the funeral, Ackworth was full of black-draped carriages as the Mayor and Corporation of Pontefract and half the carriages of Yorkshire and Durham drove in procession to the grave. They were followed by an immense concourse of gentry and tradesmen, all anxious to pay their tributes to the extraordinary life of John Gully Esquire, champion sportsman, Member of Parliament and English country gentleman.

When Gully died his estate was valued at around £70,000, equivalent to about £8m today, although that may well have been an underestimate given the extent of his business investments. He left £500 per annum to his wife Mary, £4,000 to his three married daughters, £2,000 to his son Richard and £1,000 to William. A sum of £10,000 was bequeathed for the further development of the Wingate colliery.

The will also indicates that Gully had not entirely lost contact with a brother and sister of his, Richard and Elizabeth, and he left a small amount of money to each of them. Interestingly, Richard had been a butcher by profession, and seems to have been rather more successful at the job than John!

The executors of the will were John's wife Mary, his former betting partner Harry Hall, William Armstrong, the manager of the Wingate colliery, and Thomas Belk, a solicitor and son-in-law.

Sadly, his former home at Ackworth Park suffered from subsidence and has had to be pulled down. It is now a ruin.

The burial ground besides the church has also become a rather poor memorial to such a man. He now lies in a somewhat distressed plot of land with his second wife, Mary, and two of his daughters, surrounded by a rusty wrought iron fence and rarely visited.

But he has not been entirely forgotten. In the 1975 film version of *Royal Flush*, one of George MacDonald Fraser's books in his Flashman Papers, Otto von Bismarck is manoeuvred by Flashman into boxing against a professional boxer – John Gully, who is played by Henry Cooper in the scene. More recently, in 2011 Gully was inducted into the International Boxing Hall of Fame in recognition of his fame as a bare-knuckle fighter. And at Ackworth, the village Heritage Group continues to do what it can to preserve the memories of him and his family.

When all is said and done, it is difficult not to admire John Gully. Rising from a poor butcher's son to the wealthy Squire of Ackworth Hall, he can be seen as a classic representative of the new rising middle class of Victorian England. He would have been proud of what he had achieved but was never self-satisfied or content to rest on his laurels. He loved a gamble, took some hard knocks and enjoyed the sheer excitement of success. When he died it seemed that all sporting England mourned his passing.

Short Bibliography

Allen, Jack. *The Bristol Boys*. Redcliffe Press. Bristol 2009

Ashton, John. *The History of Gambling in England*. Duckworth & Co. London 1898

Birley, Derek. *Sport and the Making of Britain*. Manchester University Press. Manchester 1993

Chinn, Carl. *Better Betting with a Decent Feller*. Aurum Press. London 2004

Curzon, Louis. *A Mirror of the Turf*. Chapman and Hall. London 1892

Darwin, Bernard. *John Gully and his Times*. Cassell & Co. London 1935

Day, William. *Reminiscences of the Turf*. Richard Bentley & Sons. London 1886

Downs Miles, Henry. *Puglistica*. Weldon. London 1880

Dixon, Henry (The Druid). *The Post and the Paddock*. Rogerson and Tuxford. London 1886

Foulkes, Nicholas. *Gentlemen and Blackguards*. Weidenfeld & Nicholson. London 2010

Greville, Charles. *The Greville Memoirs 1814-1860*. Ed. Edward Pearce. Pimlico. London 2006

Huggins, Mike. *Flat Racing and British Society 1790-2014*. Frank Cass. London 2000

Humphreys, A. L. *Crockford's*. Hutchinson, London 1953

Journals Kept by Mr. Gully and Capt. Denham During a Captivity in China in the Year 1842. Chapman and Hall. London 1844

Longrigg, Roger. *The History of Horse Racing*. MacMillan. London 1972

Pierce, Egan. *Boxiana*. Adamant Media Corp. 2006. (Facsimile of edition published by George Virtue. London 1830)

   Sporting Anecdotes. Sherword, Neely, Jones & Co. London 1820

Seth-Smith, Michael. *John Gully*. Stud and Stable. Vol.4. January 1956

   Lord Paramount of the Turf. Faber & Faber. London 1971

Sylvanus. *The Bye Lanes and Downs of England*. Richard Bentley. London 1859

Thormanby (Dixon W.) *Sporting Stories*. Mills and Boon. London 1909

   Famous Racing Men. James Hogg. London 1882

   Kings of the Turf. Hutchinson & Co. London 1898

Whyte, James. *History of the British Turf*. Henry Colburn. London 1840

Index

Ackworth Church, 170
Ackworth Park, 151-153, 159, 161-162, 187-188
Alderson, Baron, 145-146

Bare Knuckle Fighting (Pugilism), 18-29
Barclay, Captain Robert, 11-12
Belcher, Jim, 30-37
Bentinck, Lord George, 55, 74, 86, 133-140
Betting, 61-64
Blacklegs, 67-69
Bland, Jemmy, 71-73
Bond, Ludlow, 73
Bookmaking, 65-67
Bradyll, Colonel, 174
Bristol, City, 11-12
Broughton, Jack, 20-21
Buckingham, James Silk, 7-9

Cardenio, 82-83
Chifney, Sam, 60-61
Clarence, Duke of, 34, 81
Cloves, Jerry, 71
Cocken Hall, 173
Cribb, Tom, 22, 25, 31

Crockford, William, 87-99
Crockford's Club, 89-91

Danebury, Hampshire, 124-128
Davis, William, 75-76
Dawson, Daniel, 61
Day, (Honest) John, 56, 59, 80
Day, Sam, 130
Day, William, 128-129
Denham, Captain Frank, 165-166, 170
Derby, Earl of, 55
Doncaster, 54
Dunstable, 42-43
Durham Coalfields, 172-174

East India Company, 164
Edwards, Harry, 60
Epsom Downs, 51, 142

Fancy, The, 22-23, 36
Figg, James, 19-20
Fleet Street Prison, 14-15
Fletcher-Reid, 31-32, 33
Foley, Lord, 81, 84
Formosa (Taiwan), 165
Friendly Societies, 159

Gregson, Bob, 38-46
Greville, Charles, 85-86, 138
Goodman, Abraham, 142, 146
Goodym Barmby, 186-7
Gully, Mary (Polly), 154-157
Gully, John, birth 11;
    early years and marriage to
        Mary Mealing 12-13;
    London 14;
    bankruptcy and
        imprisonment, 14-15;
    fights with Pearce 33-35;
    his two fights with Gregson
        38-45;
    retires from the Ring as
        Champion of England
        45-46;
    begins life as a bookmaker
        78-82; racehorse owner
        82-84;
    becomes successful
        bookmaker 77, 80-87;
    in 1822 his first wife dies
        83;
    feud with Crockford 88-89;
    partnership with Ridsdale
        100-110;
    Member of Parliament 111-
        122;
    Danebury, Harry Hill and
        classic triumphs 123-
        128;
    the Running Rein
        conspiracy 141-147;
    retires from the Turf 132;
    marries Mary Lacey, and
        family life at Ackworth
        151-158;

    tragic loss of son Robert
        163-171;
    successful colliery owner
        and investor 172-181;
    death and funeral 186-188;
    estate 187;
    assessment of 182-188
Gully, Robert, 163-171

Hardy, John, MP, 118-121
Hetton Colliery, 174-177
Hill, Harry, 73-74, 85, 161
Horse racing, 48-64
House of Commons, 116-118

Jackson, *Gentleman* John, 21,
    28, 32
Jockey Club, 80, 133, 136

Lacey Family, 149-150
Lacey, Mary, 98, 149-152, 187-
    188
Litchwald Brothers, 146

Marwell Hall, 161-162
Mellish, Colonel Henry, 31, 32,
    35, 62, 83
Milton, Lord, 7
Mameluke, 95-99
Mealing, Mary, 14, 36, 78, 83,
    149

Newmarket, 50, 52, 79-80

O'Connell, Daniel, 117
Ogden, William, 66
Osbaldestone, Squire George,
    84, 138, 159

Payne, George, 82
Pearce, Henry, *the Game Chicken,* 16-17, 30-37
Pedley, Thomas, 126
Pierce, Egan, 30-31, 87
Plough Tavern, 36, 47, 79
Pollington, Viscount, 114-115
Pontefract Election, 113-116

Queensberry, Marquess of, 29

Railways, 53
Ridsdale, Robert, 86, 100-110
Robinson, Jem, 70-71, 147
Running Rein Conspiracy, 141-147

Smith, William, 174
Swindell, Fred, 76-77

Tattersall, Richard, 52, 63,
Thornhill, Squire, 37
Thornley Colliery, 177-180

Upper Hare Park, Newmarket, 83-84, 151

Vernon, Captain, 66

Wingate Colliery, 181
Wood, Alexander, 145-146